Race, Gender, and Identity

Race, Gender, and Identity

A Social Science Comparative Analysis of Africana Culture

James L. Conyers, Jr., editor

Africana Studies, Volume 5

Transaction Publishers
New Brunswick (U.S.A.) and London (U.K.)

Library of Congress Catalog Number: 2013010765
ISBN: 978-1-4128-5263-0
Printed in the United States of America

Library of Congress Cataloging-in-Publication Data

Race, gender, and identity : a social science comparative analysis of Africana culture / James L. Conyers, Jr., editor.
    pages cm. -- (Africana studies ; 5)
  Includes bibliographical references and index.
  ISBN 978-1-4128-5263-0 (acid-free paper)
  1. African Americans--Social conditions. 2. United States--Race relations. I. Conyers, James L.
  E185.86.R236 2013
  305.896'073--dc23
                                                        2013010765

Contents

1   Introduction: Race, Gender, and Identity   1
    James L. Conyers, Jr.

2   Conjurin' Up an Image: African American Healing   7
    Women in the Films of Julie Dash and Kasi Lemmons
    Kameelah Martin

3   African American Males' Maladaptive Coping   19
    Strategies to Racism at Predominately White
    Postsecondary Institutions
    Toya Roberts

4   They Fought a Good Fight: SNCC and Civil Rights   37
    in Mississippi
    Rochelle Brock

5   Dayton Funk Music: The Layering of Multiple Identities   51
    Portia K. Maultsby

6   The Suppression of the African Slave Trade: 57
    A Reflexive Analysis of Structural Functionalism
    and Cultural Relevance
    James L. Conyers, Jr.

7   The Big Bad Wolf: Lupus, Identity, and African   65
    American Women
    Kesha Morant Williams and Ronald L. Jackson II

8   *Steele* and the Supreme Court's Creation of the   81
     Union's Duty of Fair Representation
     Ronald Turner

9   Our Fate or Our Future: The Hip Hop Nation and   95
     Alternative Intentional Communities for Social Justice
     Lisbeth Gant-Britton

Contributors   111

Index   113

1

Introduction:
Race, Gender, and Identity

James L. Conyers, Jr.

Reflexive of the climate and culture of race in contemporary times, Africana phenomena is faced with a vexing and perplexed outcome assessment of social inequality. Progressively, this idea extends query concerning, acquisition of: autonomy, equity, agency, and sovereignty of African continental and disaporic communities. Equally important, Richard T. Schaefer exerts effort, outlining a systematic analysis of the creation and consequence of subordinate group status, in four ways: 1. Colonialism; 2. Annexation; 3. Voluntary Migration; and 4. Involuntary Migration.[1] Indeed, this structural perspective provides a base, for the context and clarification of this volume.

Withal from a cursory range, I will offer operating descriptions of the terms: race, gender, and identity. First, the term race will encumber the concept, idea, formation, and structure of the aforementioned. Secondly, the term Gender, will be defined and then contextualized, with reference to a deep cultural analysis of Africana Womanism. Lastly, the term identity is cited, to describe and evaluate a categorical and etymological variable, which is contextualized within the cultural paradigm of Africana Philosophy.

Truly, one can experiment, requisite, and develop structural expressions of the concept of race. All the same, there are few scholars, who have attempted to examine phenomena of difference from a cultural perspective of continuity, retention, and creative aspect. Essentially, volume five is a composition, which attempts to examine Race, Gender, and Identity. The essays aggregated muse a social science, humanistic, and interdisciplinary overture to Africana phenomena. Furthermore, the contributors have adopted mixed methods and meta-theory tools of analysis, to describe and evaluate events, issues, and occurrences from an African centered perspective.

Affirmatively, Schaefer, tenders a comprehensive definition of race, which can be assorted in two-fold manner of: 1. Biological and 2. Social Significance.[2] Furthermore, Allen Jonson outlines the concept and social construction of race, as: Race can be interpreted as: grouping or classification based on genetic variations in physical appearance, most notably in skin color.[3] Accessorially, I proffer, Consequently, race is fixed contemporary times as a category of literature, repeatedly employing assimilations' theories.[4] Ensuant, Oscar Gandy yields an assessment of race composing: Race is a theoretical construct. It is a product of the realm of ideas, thought, reflection, and perhaps even imagination. Its meaning is negotiated or, as many prefer, contested because of the ways in which that meaning has been linked historically to the distribution of life chances.[5] For a cultivating assessment, with regard to a composition of racism and culture, Frantz Fanon writes:

> The unilaterally decreed normative value of certain cultures deserves our careful attention. One of the paradoxes immediately encountered is the rebound of egocentric, sociocentric definitions. There is first affirmed the existence of human groups having not culture, then of a hierarchy of cultures, and finally, the concept of cultural relativity.
>
> We have here the whole range from overall negation to singular and specific recognition. It is precisely this fragmented and bloody history that we must sketch on the level of cultural anthropology.[6]

Still, the use of the term Gender pertains to a differential between men and women. Notwithstanding, the source is referential to examining the consequences of creating subordinate group status. Advancing onward to describing the term Gender, Schaefer, posits the following:

> Gender roles are society's expectations regarding the proper behavior, attitudes, and activities of males and females. Toughness has traditionally been seen in the United States as masculine—and desirable only in men—while tenderness has been viewed a feminine. A society may require that one sex or the other take the primary responsibility for the socialization of the children, economic support of the family, or religious leadership.[7]

With emphasis on Africana Womanism, the term has been adjusted to reference and resource, the study of Africana communities to define gender and the specificity as related to the Black community. Substantively, the discussion of disparity, with emphasis on gender, requires alternative query and sources, extended outside the binary analysis of gender types.

Shirley Moody-Turner and James B. Stewart vignette Anna Julia Cooper, as a cultural motif, compiling:

> In 1886, at the age of twenty-eight, Anna Julia Cooper stood before the black male clergy of the Protestant Episcopal Church and argued that the issues affecting black women and poor and working-class African Americans needed to be placed at the center of racial uplift efforts. The image of the young but resolute Cooper standing at the center of a male-dominated space, representing the needs and perspectives of black women and the working poor, creates an apt metaphor for illustrating the importance of Cooper's place in the development of Africana studies.[8]

Likewise, Nikol G. Alexander-Floyd and Evelyn M. Simien supplement this discussion further, by mentioning:

> Although Africana womanism is a growing academic and political identification, scholars have yet to adequately explore its relationship to Black feminism. Current interest in whether various types of Black women's intellectual production should be named womanism or Black feminism mirrors the pre-occupation with questions of individual versus group identity and crosscutting versus consensus issues that take place within Black civil society today. While some scholars conflate womanism and Black feminism, others insist the two are inherently incompatible.[9]

Adjacently, the term identity, with emphasis on Africana phenomena designates world view and culture. Indeed, cosmology lends discussion to interpretation, context, and defining reality, based on historical and cultural experiences. Finely, Lucius Outlaw provides a working analysis of the term Africana Philosophy:

> "Africana philosophy" is the phrase I use as a "gathering" notion under which to situate the articulations (writings, speeches, etc.), and traditions of the same, of Africans and peoples of African descent collectively, as well as the sub-discipline- or field-forming, tradition-defining, tradition organizing reconstructive efforts which are (to be) regarded as philosophy. Use of the qualifier "Africana" is consistent with the practice of grouping and identifying intellectual traditions and practices by the national, geo graphic, cultural, racial, and/or ethnic name for the persons who initiated and were or are the primary prac-titioners - and/or are the subjects and objects - of the practices and traditions in question (e.g., "American," "British," "French," "German," or "continental" philosophy).[10]

Furthermore, Maulana Karenga extends this discussion by writing:

> Kawaida critically examines various contributions to Black and human history, and makes a selective analysis of what is real and relevant, extracts it, integrates it into its

system and then, puts it in the service of Black liberation. It is a process historically established. Nothing comes into being by itself; every person and thought draws and rises from the social-historical context to which they owe their existence.[11]

Additionally, Kwame Nkrumah remarks about this phenomena, with reference to Consciencism, in the following:

> According to philosophical consciencism, ethical rules are not permanent but depend on the stage reached in the historical evolution of a society, so however, that cardinal principles of egalitarianism are conserved. A society does not change its ethics by merely changing its rules. To alter its ethics its princisples must be different. Thus, if a capitalist society can become a socialist society, then a capitalist society will have changed its ethics. Any change of ethics constitutes a revolutionary change.[12]

Hence, the survey descriptors examine thematic emphasis of this volume which center on race, gender, and identity. Moreover, the emphasis on the subtitle of a social science analysis, lends itself, for providing an interdisciplinary matrix of examining phenomena from an alternative lens. Equally important, Ruth Reviere provides an interesting analysis which is noted as,

> New orientations to the acquisition and use of data are necessary because the pertinent literature are virtually silent on the views of African and other non-European communities, dealing almost exclusively with Eurocentric scholars whose interpretations are inevitably colored by European views of the phenomena being studied. These new Afrocentric methodologies are intended to be used to investigate pertinent research questions legitimately and effectively (that is, truthfully and inclusively), especially those that possess embedded assumptions about race and culture.[13]

The aforementioned points of reference, regarding race can be referred to as, the study of doctrines, which address the physical and cultural differential of a people. Moreover, race is primarily a socially constructed variable. On the other hand, there is coding and interpreting of this biological determinant, from a cultural or structural analysis.

Ensuant, in the editing and preparation of this volume, emphasis was drawn on the ascription, aggregation, and research cluster of essays, with emphasis on Race, Gender, and Identity. Indeed, the topic is familiar, however, the approach and context of each essay provides a fresh analysis of variables, with description and evaluation of the aforementioned phenomena. First, Kameelah Martin extends a critical study, probing Julie Dash and Kasi Lemmons film work, through a literary gridiron of African American literature, in the way of the Healing Woman. Martin's appraisal relinquishes an alternative interpretation of Africana retention and traditions.

Toya Roberts offers an empirical ethnographic study of African American males at predominantly white institutions of higher education. Grounded within a structural format, the author deposits query and variables, regarding the frequency of: stress, attrition, retention, and performance. Her use of qualitative research tools, provide an alternate lens to review the phenomena. Additionally, Rochelle Brocks survey analysis of the Student Non-Violent Coordinating Committee in nexus to the Civil Rights movement, usurps the transition, transformation, and transcendence of the Black Arts/Black Power movements, and the lasting contributions of the Post Civil Rights era.

Portia Maultsby engages an ethnographic study, inspecting the genre of Funk Music in the United States. In an historical perspective, Maultsby gathers threads of the intellectual precedents of Black music, reflected within the cultural comforter of Africana identity. James L. Conyers, Jr., offers a reflexive analysis centered on structural functionalism and cultural relevance, with emphasis on using W.E.B. DuBois study of the *Suppression of the African Slave Trade*, as a rubric for a descriptive and evaluative study, regarding Africana phenomena.

The co-authored essay contributed by Kesha M. Williams and Ronald L. Jackson, II, sequesters issues centered on identity and Africana womanism. Thus, emphasis is on the disease of Lupus. The co-authors employ Grounded Theory and Participant Observation, to describe and evaluate the diagnosis and medical prognosis of African Americans living with the disease. Ronald Turner's essay on the *Steele* and Supreme Court decision, is a narrative historical reviewing the legal strategy of Charles H. Houston and his co-counsel, regarding African Americans intrigue and dextral autonomy, pertaining to union representation of the Brotherhood of Locomotive Firemen and Enginemen. Lisbeth Gant Britton renders a conceptual history probing the posture, position, and placement of the Hip Hop community, with emphasis on international issues and schema. The idea of social justice renders dialog pertaining to disparity, racism, and discrimination. Still situated within a dual labor economy, the author offers alternative options from literary canons as correctives for the advancement of systemic subordination African American. Finally, in the spirit of the Africana intellectual tradition of social science enquiry, this volume endeavors to nominate a singular contribution, regarding the advancement of research and writing of: race, gender and identity, with emphasis on the Africana continental experience.

Notes

1. Richard T. Schafer. *Racial and Ethnic Groups* (New York: HarperCollins College Publishers, 6th edition, 1996), 3–15.
2. Richard T. Schaefer, *Racial and Ethnic Groups* (New York: HarperCollins College Publishers, 6th edition, 1996), 12–14.
3. Allen G. Johnson, *The Blackwell Dictionary of Sociology* (Cambridge, MA: Blackwell, 1995), 223.
4. James L. Conyers, Jr., *Black Cultures and Race Relations* (Chicago: Burnham Inc. Publishers, 2002), 276.
5. Oscar H. Gandy, Jr., *Communication and Race: A Structural Perspective* (New York: Oxford University Press, 1998), 35.
6. Franz Fanon, "Racism and Culture," in *I Am Because We Are*, edited by Fred L. Hord and Jonathan S. Lee, 172. University of Massachusetts Press, 1995.
7. Richard T. Schaefer, *Racial and Ethnic Groups* (New York: HarperCollins College Publishers, 6th edition, 1996), 431.
8. Shirley Moody-Turner and James B. Stewart. "Gendering Africana Studies: Insights from Anna Julia Cooper." *African American Review* 34, no. 1, (Spring 2008): 35.
9. Nikol G. Alexander-Floyd and Evelyn M. Simien. "Revisiting 'What's in a Name?': Exploring the Contours of Africana Womanist Thought." *Frontiers: A Journal of Women Studies* 27, no. 1 (2006): 67.
10. Lucius Outlaw, "Africana Philosophy." *The Journal of Ethics* 1, no. 3 (1997): 267.
11. Maulana Karenga, "Kawaida and Its Critics: A Sociohistorical Analysis." *Journal of Black Studies* 8, no. 2 (December 1977): 139.
12. Kwame Nkrumah, "Consciencism," *I Am Because We Are*, edited by Fred Lee Hord and Jonathan S. Lee, 56. Cambridge, Massachusetts: University of Massachusetts Press, 1995.
13. Ruth Reviere, "Toward an Afrocentric Research Methodology" *Journal of Black Studies* 31, no. 6, (July 2001): 709.

2

Conjurin' Up an Image:
African American Healing Women in the
Films of Julie Dash and Kasi Lemmons

Kameelah Martin

In the latter half of the twentieth century such African American authors as Toni Morrison, Gloria Naylor, Arthur Flowers, and Alice Walker have rewritten African American healing, or conjure, women in a way that honors and appreciates their existence rather than degrades and trivializes it. Rather than being relegated to Eurocentric stereotypes of witches, devil-worshippers, and cannibals, Morrison and her contemporaries have returned the literary conjure woman to her reverent status. Pilate Dead, Miranda Day, Tante Rosie, and Melvira Dupree all spring from a postmodern tradition of writers who mean to reappropriate and reinstate the conjure woman as a folk hero specific to the history of African people in the New World. The movement toward reclamation of the conjure woman and the alternate spirituality of African American women, however, is not confined to the literary world. As Akasha Gloria Hull points out, "In public media such as television and film, black women are playing a strong role in conveying spiritual themes and material" (2001, 152). Hull encourages critics and scholars to look outside of the literary circuit to get a fuller picture of what is taking place in black women's spirituality, arguing that looking "at these media phenomena extends our exploration of this new spirituality into arenas that are equally as important as lived experience and books" (2001, 152).

Rather than being depicted exclusively in the work of African American authors, the conjure woman's character has spilled over into the realm of film, most notably in *The Believers* (Schlesinger 1987), *Daughters of the Dust* (Dash 1991), *Midnight in the Garden of Good and Evil* (Eastwood 1997), *Eve's Bayou* (Lemmons 1997), *Caught Up* (Scott 1998), and more recently in *The Skeleton Key* (Softley 2005) and *Pirates of the Caribbean: Dead Man's Chest* (Verbinski 2006). The portrayal of the conjure woman in these films moves from gross stereotype to reverence and even teeters on ambivalence in some cases. This essay seeks to place the genres of film and literature in conversation with each other to explore the representation of the conjure woman figure in the popular imagination. While the films by Schlesinger, Eastwood, Scott, Softley, and Verbinski provide a pool of resources for examining the conjure woman figure in film, the scope of my inquiry is limited and very specific. Of particular importance to this project are the ways in which African American filmmakers reconstruct the image of "Sistah Conjurer," to borrow Valerie Lee's phrase, engaging issues of body politics, stereotype, and the position of African retentions in visual texts (1996, 1). I take as my subject the films of Julie Dash and Kasi Lemmons, whose work reflects the lives and physicality of conjure women as African American female filmmakers conceive them, to ponder the critical questions: (1) Do visual representations of conjure women help or hinder the project of reclamation and cultural preservation that has taken place in contemporary African American literature? (2) Do the films *Daughters of the Dust* and *Eve's Bayou* offer a safe space for the conjure woman to exist in visual culture? Both films are woman-centered and highlight conjuring communities. As such, they provide a rich land-scape in which to thoroughly explore the nuanced, filmic representation of the African American woman healer.

Film plays a critical role in the quest of recovering the conjure woman from the depths of cultural intolerance, degradation, and ignorance. The written word is limited in the ways it can shape one's perception, understanding, and articulation of what and who the conjure woman is. The visual image, however, resonates more strongly, ingraining someone else's concept in the mind of a willing audience. Much like the conjure tradition, visual media engages in both healing and harmful practices.[1] It can restore damaged, inaccurate images to their past glory or perpetuate prejudiced, stigmatized ideals that become more difficult to challenge. The visual images of healing women in Julie Dash's *Daughters of the Dust* (1991) and Kasi Lemmons's *Eve's Bayou* (1997) must be assessed to determine whether the film portrayals of African American spiritual healers continue to pay homage to and reshape the conjure woman across genres within her own cultural matrix.

Dash and Lemmons—two black, female, independent filmmakers—prove themselves committed to ideals of challenging and reappropriating the image of the conjure woman in an overtly conscious way. Lemmons revitalizes the conjure woman's physical image three times over in the most successful independent film of 1997. *Eve's Bayou* is "an original and historically respectful exploration of diverse African American spiritual traditions, which tackles, in a deft and sophisticated manner, such femininely resonant topics as sexual abuse and the possibilities of personal freedom for women" (Hull 2001, 198). Set in 1962 Louisiana, the storyline has a glaring resemblance to Gloria Naylor's *Mama Day* (1988). The story surrounds the Batiste family, descendants of the slave healer Eve who was bequeathed a sizable amount of land by her master, the southern aristocrat General Jean-Paul Batiste, after she cured him of cholera. Eve populated the land with sixteen of Batiste's children and the land took on her name, appropriately called Eve's Bayou. Much like the descendants of Sapphira Wade, the living Batistes are a family of healers. Louis Batiste (Samuel L. Jackson) is the local physician, who does little more than "push aspirin to the elderly," while his sister Mozelle (Debbi Morgan) is a "psychic counselor," tending to the otherworldly needs of the community (Lemmons 1998, 189, 166). Then there is young Eve (Journee Smollett), the most recent of the Batiste descendants to inherit her slave ancestor's gift of second sight.

In defiance of all stereotypes and preconceived notions as to which images black women should be confined, Lemmons certainly depicts her conjure women against the grain. Mozelle Batiste, to whom the audience is introduced early in the film, is stunningly beautiful. She has long, flowing, unprocessed, red hair, contrary to popular beliefs that black women "barely [have] enough [hair] to wash, let alone press and curl" (Collins 2000, 91). She is glamorous, wearing beaded gowns, jewelry, and high-heeled shoes in many of her scenes—a reflection of her middle-class status. Mozelle is obviously attractive to men as evidenced by her three marriages and pending romance with Julian Gray-Raven, yet she is not overtly sexualized. Her lips are painted red through most of the film, calling attention to their suppleness and marking her as a sexual being, but she is not captured in any lewd, deviant sex acts. In *Black Feminist Thought* Patricia Hill Collins discusses the characteristics of the cult of true womanhood—piety, purity, submissiveness, and domesticity—which she argues are used to fuel the controlling, oppressive images of black women.[2] Mozelle's sexuality, rather than reflecting the image of the sexually aggressive, promiscuous Jezebel that Collins describes, strikes a healthy balance between the purity/asexuality of the cult of true womanhood and the indiscriminate nature of so-called "loose" women. Mozelle explains to her niece Eve, with no sense of shame or embarrassment, that her extra-marital lover, Hosea, lit a fire under her that even her husband at the time, Maynard, could not quell. This is a woman who is very comfortable with her sexuality and one who, perhaps, reflects a more tangible idea of black women's sexuality than Jezebel or Mammy ever has. Not only does Mozelle defy the association with long-standing ideas about black women's sexual appetites, but she also removes herself from domestic space.

There are no scenes in which Mozelle is chopping vegetables, boiling water, washing dishes, or otherwise preparing the family meal. She is conspicuously absent from the Sunday brunch attended by all the other Batiste relatives. She admittedly has neither children nor the responsibilities of motherhood. She smokes cigarettes and moves about as she sees fit, ever outside of the domesticity in which her mother and sister-in-law, Roz (Lynn Whitfield), exist. In contrast, the eldest conjurer in the neighborhood, Elzora (Diahann Carroll) is pictured in the kitchen sharing a bowl of gumbo with Eve during the ten-year-old's initial consultation with the hoodoo lady. Elzora's placement in the kitchen, however, does not automatically confer unto her the history and embodiment of the domestic worker or mammy figure. She obviously makes her living through her spiritual prowess by divining the future for those so inclined to know at the local farmer's market, rather than cleaning the homes of wealthy white people. While it is unknown whether Elzora has any children, the film does make it clear that she lives alone and, thus, has no domestic obligations to anyone besides herself.

While Elzora does not fit easily into any of the common black female stereotypes, casting Diahann Carroll as the aged conjurer proved to be a challenge for Lemmons. In the director's commentary on the film, Lemmons admits that the producers were not convinced that Carroll was the right fit for the role because she was "too beautiful." The suggestion here is that conjuring and beauty are antithetical; any woman dealing in African-steeped secrets of the supernatural is automatically assumed unattractive and haggardly. Common associations with women and magic evoke images of the classic, Eurocentric witch—old, gray, wrinkled, and complete with a large nose and missing teeth. Presumably, this is the image that the film producers were conjuring up in relation to Elzora's character. Lemmons's film, however, insists that conjure women do not have to reflect the dominant culture's supposition that remnants of an African past are grotesque. The film does not depict any romantic interests for Elzora, but there are other telling signs that indicate that her attractiveness and sexuality have not been erased due to her occupation, age, or race.

During Eve's return visit to Elzora's reclusive home to retrieve the voodoo doll she assumes is part of the death spell she has requested, the hoodoo lady answers the door in a long cotton nightgown that suggestively falls off her bare shoulders. Her silvery gray hair is also hanging to its full length. While such signs may appear unsubstantial, I argue that Elzora's loose hair and bare shoulders are cinematic cliché for sexual awareness and desirability. I do not mean to suggest that Elzora is exerting her sexual energy toward Eve, only that she is obviously aware and comfortable with her sexuality and wears her desirability effortlessly—even with age. Lemmons brilliantly challenges her audiences' perception of what a conjure woman should be, demonstrating through Elzora that the conjurer is not a type or a static image but rather a fluid one, ever changing and appearing in places viewers are not prepared to look.

The characters of *Eve's Bayou* confront preconceived notions of conjure women as old, gray, and wrinkled or big, black, and fat. Both Mozelle and Elzora subvert long-standing correlations between conjure and hoodoo—often referred to as black magic—with something vile, ugly, and unsightly. Conversely, the conjure women of Lemmons's imagination have unparalleled beauty even in their weakest and darkest moments. Even young Eve, the conjure novice, is innocently beautiful. Lemmons's portrayal teaches the audience that these women, so-called heathens, devil-worshippers, and the like, are more human than perhaps previously thought. Mozelle, Elzora, and Eve resemble the common folk; they represent familiar and safe images to the black spectator.

Julie Dash also consciously manipulates the visual image of Nana Peazant, the conjuring figure in *Daughters of the Dust*. As the eighty-eight-year-old matriarch of the Peazant clan, Nana represents the oldest living connection to the African past for Ibo Landing. Dash was very much invested in visibly recognizing Nana's reverence of the old ways as well as her role as nurturing ancestor. It becomes clear in her casting choice, however, that she was not interested in perpetuating the robust, jolly, black woman of Southern myth. Rather, Nana (Cora Lee Day) is a slender-framed, dark-complexioned woman with strong ethnic features. Nana has a very sharp and distinct facial bone structure. She has a gap between her teeth, rumored to be a sign of beauty in many African cultures, while her dark skin represents her ties to Africa, a cherished and honored connection among the Geechee community of Dash's creation.

The celebration of darker skin and Africanness is not only reflected in the aesthetic "revisioning [of] the cinematic iconography of black women" throughout the film, Dash also reiterates the beauty and power of the darker hued in *Daughters of the Dust: A Novel* (1997), which returns to Ibo Landing several years after the Peazants "crossover" to the mainland (Machiorlatti 2005, 98). When Amelia, the light-skinned granddaughter of Haagar Peazant returns to the island to study her Geechee relatives, her skin is a mark of disdain:

> Every now and then, one of her fellow travelers glanced back at Amelia and touched their chest. . . . Elizabeth had also noticed the gesture, the touching of the protective charm that everyone wore under their clothes. She chided herself for not remembering how suspicious people were of "red-bone" people. Cousin Amelia with her brown hair and red-brown coloring would have much to overcome. (Dash 1997, 68–69)

Rather than praising and privileging lighter skin, Dash deliberately situates Amelia as the "exoticized Other," the anomaly in a world where dark skin is the standard of beauty. Dash pushes the envelope even further as Amelia voices her discomfort and self-consciousness at the way her skin color determines others' attitude toward her:

> When Amelia had first recognized the charm-touching gesture for what it was, she had been amused. But now, it irritated her, for she saw it as an ignorant habit that emphasized the difference between her and the others. It hurt her, and for the first time in her life, her color was not an advantage among her own people. (1997, 95)

Amelia is getting a small glimpse of the prejudice that is often experienced over a lifetime for people of African descent with deep, melanin-rich skin tones. Dash's subversion of color preference biases in both the novel and the film reinforces her mission to "break with the tradition" of what Patricia Hill Collins calls the controlling images that continue to oppress black women (Dash 1992, 51).

Skin color, however, is not the only place where Nana Peazant's body politics depart from the stereotypical images associated with black women of spiritual power. Even though she is well into her eighth decade, Nana does not wear a crown of graying hair, which often represents the stress and turmoil of modern living. Viola, her granddaughter, is noticeably gray, though she seems to be only half Nana's age. She, coincidentally, has given her life over to the mainland and assimilated into a Eurocentric understanding of the world. Nana, on the other hand, lives a very simple, organic life, producing whatever food, remedies, or cosmetics necessary for survival with what can be yielded from the earth. Nana's hair is cropped short and styled in palm-rolled coils to represent her Africanist lifestyle, a representation of great import to Dash. In a conversation with bell hooks she discusses why hair was such a concern in the film:

> The hairstyles we're wearing now are based upon ancient hairstyles, and there is a tradition behind these hairstyles. They mean things. In any West African country, you know, if you were a pre-teen you have a certain hairstyle. If you were in puberty you have another hairstyle. Menopausal, another hairstyle. Married, single, whatever. All of this means something. There is so much meaning to our heritage that just goes overlooked. . . . We researched that. (Dash 1992, 53)

As Sandra M. Grayson notes in *Symbolizing the Past: Reading Sankofa, Daughters of the Dust, & Eve's Bayou as Histories* (2000), "in order to break with cliché, formula, and stereotype in representing the history of enslaved Africans in North America, Dash used numerous symbols in *Daughters of the Dust* including the figurehead of an African warrior floating in the swamp, ancient markings within drawings on the wall, and a graveyard that reflects burial practices of the Kongo" (40). Dash also took this approach in her characterization of Nana Peazant. Nana is a product and survivor of American slavery, but her body does not reveal the pain of that existence in the most recognizable ways. There are neither chains, brandings, or chokecherry tree scars on her back nor do her descendants wear the identifiable marks of a recent white progenitor in their physical appearances. In an attempt to expand the discourse on the visible signs of slavery, Dash allows the indigo-stained hands of Nana and the elder women of the community to voice their oppression. Dash explains that she was using indigo "as a symbol of slavery, [creating] a new kind of icon around slavery rather than the traditional [signs]" (Dash 1992, 31). The indigo stains not only Nana's hands but also her clothing. Rather than wearing the white cotton dresses like the other women on the island, Nana dons an indigo-dyed frock that represents the work she endured in slavery. Her dress sets her apart from the other women on the island, marking her as a character of reverence and wisdom that reaches further back in the memories of slavery and Africa than perhaps any other figure in the film. She wears her indigo dress like the robes of royalty and the symbolic message is not lost on the viewer. For Ibo Landing, Nana is the closest African ancestor still living.

As an antithetical representation of the classic mammy figure, Dash's image of the nurturing family matriarch addresses in an innovative way the asexual condition that has become synonymous with such figures. As Collins argues, asexuality is prerequisite to authentic mammy-hood. "The mammy image is one of an asexual woman, a surrogate mother in blackface whose historical devotion to her White family is now giving way to expectations" (2000, 74). Rather than depict Nana in suggestive positions or focus on memories of lovemaking with her deceased husband, Dash takes a more subtle approach to departing from the stereotype. Nana's sexuality is implied through the horde of descendants that surround her. While the number of children born to Nana is never revealed in the film or the novel, the presence of four generations of Peazants is proof enough that Mother Peazant was engaged in sexual activity.

The film solidifies that Nana's reproduction was not a result of her being "forced," to use Nana's euphemism. The film alludes to Nana's young life with her husband, Shad, in a flashback scene where a young man with ritually scarred cheeks instructs Nana on what to do with the earth running through her hands. The relationship is a very loving and affectionate one even beyond the grave, as evidenced by Nana herself, who tells her great grandson Eli (Adisa Anderson), "I visit with old Peazant every day since the day he died" (Dash 1992, 96). The marriage of the elder Peazants is an understated reference in the film, though critical in Nana's disrupting inaccurate and damaging images of black women in general and conjure women specifically. Through the subtle hints revealed in the film, Nana's coupling with Shad "was not just about lust, was not just about sex or violence or some kind of platonic, mother/grandfather type situation" as Dash informs (1992, 55). Rather, it is a loving relationship between a black man and woman. Nana and Shad Peazant enjoyed a long life together and apparently brought several children into the world. As mentioned earlier, with the exception of Yellow Mary (Barbara O.), none of the Peazant descendants appearing in the film possess the visible features of a biracial heritage so one can assume that Shad, rather than some random, lecherous, white landowner, is indeed the progenitor of the Peazant clan.

With Nana's sexuality safely intact, other parts of her being are available for analysis. As part of her faith and lifestyle, Nana is invested in the practice of African-centered spirituality. As with many other fictionalized conjure women, she too finds power in her own body.[3] Dash places great emphasis on Nana's "laying on of hands" as part of her ministry. One of the earliest images in the film is of two hands sifting through red dirt; later the viewer discovers that those hands belong to Nana. Nana has laid her hands in the soil of the island, communing with the ancestors who rest there and claiming the land as home for her descendants. The most amazing trick, however, that Nana turns with her "hand" is the "Root Revival of Love" that sends a piece of her spirit with each of her migrating descendants to protect them once they cross over to the mainland. Nana works on the "hand" throughout the single day in which the film takes place, stitching and stuffing herbs here and intertwining strands of hair there until her hoodoo charm is complete. As metaphorical as it is, the hand that Nana attaches to the Bible certainly holds a most potent power: her own and that of the ancestors whom Nana keeps close through "scraps of memory."

The power of Nana's hands is most noticeable in her interactions with one of her granddaughters. When Yellow Mary returns to the island and seeks a quiet moment with Nana, the two women share a very intimate exchange as Nana lays her healing hands on her granddaughter. "Without censure, without expectations, without judgment, Yellow Mary's grandmother strokes her hair and gazes affectionately into her face, making sure that her excursion to the New World has not destroyed her inner being. When she is satisfied that all is well, Nana Peazant leans in toward Yellow Mary and places their foreheads softly together" (Bobo 1995, 162). Nana's hands wash away any of the shame and hurt that Yellow Mary has endured since being "ruint" during her stay in Cuba. Nana's hands also help Yellow Mary to reach clarity of mind. During the scene in which Yellow Mary, her lesbian companion, Trula (Trula Hoosier), and Eula (Alva Rogers) are casually talking under the parasol they have discovered on the beach, Yellow Mary informs Eula of her future plans. "When I leave here . . . I'll be heading up for Canada. Nova Scotia. I like the sound of that place . . . Nova Scotia. . . .I never had too much trouble making a dollar. Never needed nobody to help me do that" (Dash 1992, 145). Then Yellow Mary's speech assumes a more persuasive tone, "I can't stand still. Got to keep moving. New faces, new places. . . . Nova Scotia will be good to me" (1992, 145).

While Yellow Mary is directing her comments to Eula, she is also trying to convince herself that she must keep moving to evade the emptiness that continues to haunt her. She divulges the truth of her unhappiness as she and Nana embrace a second time. Nana's hands wrap tightly around both Yellow Mary and Eula in an emotional frenzy, nudging the discontent in Yellow Mary's heart into her throat and out of her mouth for all to hear. "You know I'm not like the other women here. But I need to know that I can come home . . . to hold on to what I come from. I need to know the people here know my name. . . . I want to stay. I want to stay and visit with you here" (1992, 154). Intoxicated with the comforts of home and by Nana's touch, Yellow Mary cannot bear to part with Ibo Landing.

Daughters of the Dust, like *Eve's Bayou*, presents a very human image of Nana Peazant. She is a mother, a grandmother, a wife; she mourns the loss of her husband and cries when her family separates. She laughs a little, too. Nana is neither depicted as an aberrant citizen in her community nor a horrid, old lady who eats children. Such connotations of conjure women are simply inaccurate and used to discredit the cultural and, especially, the spiritual authority with which their communities imbued them. Dash's and Lemmons's films add a tremendous force behind the cultural preservation and retrieval of the African American healing woman from the depths of Eurocentric stigmatization. Mozelle Batiste, Elzora, Nana Peazant, and Eve are but four possible branches that stem from the rich, enduring cultural icon of the conjure woman. Dash and Lemmons bring to life the Aunt Peggys, Sapphira Wades, Indigos, and Melviras of the African American literary imagination. They capture the diversity of physical types of African American women and challenge the normative, witch-like associations forced onto conjure women like Tituba of Salem Witch Trial infamy, for instance.

The images of conjure women presented in these films are critical to the process of reappropriation because they challenge popular belief, but most importantly because these images were created by black women for other black women. Dash and Lemmons reflect conjure women who are not unlike their own mothers, grandmothers, and in Lemmons's case, her aunt.[4] These depictions, like those in the fiction of Jewell Parker Rhodes, Maryse Condè, and others, mirror the histories, legends, and lives of women who in one form or another existed and touched the lives of the directors. This is what makes them real, believable, and so invaluable to the task at hand.

"The Black Feminist narrative style" of both *Eve's Bayou* and *Daughters of the Dust* is, as Machiorlattie suggests, "one of recollection and remembering so that stereotypes can be subverted, inaccurate historical representation corrected, and new aesthetic choices and forms merge that diffuse dominant forms" (2005, 98). Lemmons and Dash's respective films are undeniably engaged in the work of black feminist criticism, challenging the place of black women in history, the imagination, and their roles in creative processes outside of the literary realm. Much like Gloria Naylor's *Mama Day;* Ntozake Shange's *Sassafrass, Cypress & Indigo*; and Paule Marshall's *Praisesong for the Widow* before them, Lemmons and Dash create narratives surrounding black women, history, and magic that give voice to a very particular cultural experience and aesthetic extending their branch of this well-established theme in African American artistic lineage from the page to the screen.

Notes

1. Because the African cosmology from which conjure evolved does not recognize such concepts as good and evil the same way Christianity does, Theophus Smith argues that rather than thinking about conjure in terms of binary oppositions, it should not be conceptualized in so limiting a view. According to the introduction of *Conjuring Culture,* conjure has the unlimited ability to both heal and harm depending on how the power is invoked and for what purpose.
2. The Cult of True Womanhood, according to Barbara Welter, is a term used to describe nineteenth-century ideals of womanhood. Welter identifies four tenants of the True Woman: (1) a woman should be pious; (2) a woman should exemplify purity of heart, mind, and especially body; (3) a true woman submits to the will and ways of one's husband; and (4) a true woman reigns over domesticity. See Welter for a full discussion of the term and its cultural reverberations. Collins discusses this idea in chapter four.
3. As I argue in my forthcoming monograph, there are other notable healing women such as Octavia Butler's Anywanwu from *Wild Seed* (1980), Lena McPherson in Tina McElroy Ansa's *Baby of the Family* (1989) and *The Hand I Fan With* (1996), and Gayl Jones's Harland Eagleton from *The Healing.* All reflect their spiritual prowess through their physical bodies. Anywanwu is a shape shifter who can use her own body to make healing salves. Lena McPherson can fix a stalled car and turn muddy water clear with the touch of her hand or body excrements. Harland Eagleton also applies her faith healing by laying hands on her subjects. The correlation between African American healers and the physical body can also be explored in the phenomenon of spirit possession, which is innately connected to the physical body. Jewell Parker Rhodes's novel *Voodoo Dreams: A Novel of Marie Laveau* (1992) focuses on healing through possession. See *Conjuring Moments in African American Literature: Women, Spirit Work, & Other Such Hoodoo.* New York: Palgrave Macmillan, forthcoming 2013.
4. The character Mozelle Batiste is based on Lemmons's Aunt Murial who also lost several husbands to mysterious circumstances, practiced divination and voodoo, and was told by another conjure woman that she was cursed as a black widow. Lemmons discusses her aunt and the creative process of creating Mozelle in the Director's Commentary, an extra feature on the DVD.

References

Bobo, Jacqueline. *Black Women as Cultural Readers.* New York: Columbia University Press, 1995.

Collins, Patricia Hill. *Black Feminist Thought: Knowledge, Consciousness, and the Politics of Empowerment.* 2nd ed. New York: Routledge, 2000.

Dash, Julie. *Daughters of the Dust: A Novel.* New York: Plume, 1997.

————. *Daughters of the Dust: The Making of an African American Women's Film.* New York: The New Press, 1992.

Daughters of the Dust. DVD. Directed by Julie Dash. Performed by Cora Lee Day, Barbara O., and Adisa Anderson. Kino International, 1991.

Daughters of the Dust:Director's Audio Commentary. DVD. Directed by Julie Dash. Kino International, 1999.

Eve's Bayou. DVD. Directed by Kasi Lemmons. Performed by Samuel L. Jackson, Lynn Whitfield, Diahann Carroll, and Journee Smollett. Lion's Gate, 1997.

Eve's Bayou: Commentary with Cast and Director. DVD. Lion's Gate, 2002.

Grayson, Sandra. *Symbolizing the Past: Reading Sankofa, Daughters of the Dust, and Eve's Bayou as Histories.* Lanham, MD: University Press of America, 2000.

Hull, Akasha Gloria. *Soul Talk: The New Spirituality of African American Women.* Rochester, VT: Inner Traditions, 2001.

Lee, Valerie. *Granny Midwives and Black Women Writers: Double-Dutched Readings.* New York: Routledge, 1996.

Lemmons, Kasi. "Eve's Bayou: Screenplay." *Scenario: The Magazine of Screenwriting Art* 4.2 (Summer 1998): 153–91.

Machiorlatti, Jennifer. "Revisiting Julie Dash's Daughters of the Dust: Black Feminist Narrative and Diasporic Recollection." *South Atlantic Review* 70, no. 1 (Winter 2005): 97–116.

Smith, Theophus. *Conjuring Culture: Biblical Formations of Black America.* New York: Oxford University Press, 1994.

Welter, Barbara. "The Cult of True Womanhood: 1820–1860." *American Quarterly* 18, no. 2 Part i (Summer1966): 151–174.

3

African American Males' Maladaptive Coping Strategies to Racism at Predominately White Postsecondary Institutions

Toya Roberts

Introduction

As the number of African Americans gaining admission and enrolling into postsecondary institutions of higher education continues to increase, it is important to note that the majority of these students will attend institutions in which the campus population is predominately White. Research has found that on these campuses African Americans are experiencing significantly negative side effects associated with social isolation and alienation (Pascarella and Terenzini 1991; Haralson 1995). Research

---

To My Readers: I need to start this brief article with a disclaimer. I am not a historian. I am a teacher educator with a passion to read and learn more about the Civil Rights Movement. I am a teacher of teachers who uses cultural studies to understand or analyze issues. I am a Black woman who wants to better understand my people's history and especially our fight for equal rights and what we need to do in the present to build on the successes and mistakes of the past. I used a handful of articles—albeit great articles, in my humble opinion—to begin to understand what I see as an exciting time in history and, importantly, to understand how this knowledge can be used in my teacher education classes.

has also indicated that most African American college students attending Predominately White Institutions (PWIs) leave by their sophomore year (Haralson 1995).

Because racism and practices of exclusion still have a negative impact on African American males on college campuses (Harris 1996), how they cope with the stresses of these environments warrants important consideration. "At minimum, Black men carry the burden of two negative social identities as they move through society, one as a member of the African American race (i.e., anti-Black racism and stereotypes) and the other as a Black male (i.e., Black misandry or anti-Black male ideologies, stereotypes, and oppression)" (Smith, Hung, and Franklin 2011, 66). Consequently, Black men are constantly developing unique racial and gendered, race-based techniques for applying adaptive or maladaptive coping strategies to racism (Harris 1996; Smith et al. 2011).

PWIs provide settings that are useful to examine the influence of such factors as prejudice and racism on academic outcomes both within and outside of the school environment (Davis 1994). Additionally, a number of studies suggest that two leading factors differentially affect Black college student educational attainment at PWIs: (1) a perceived lack of positive social support; and (2) perceived discrimination on the part of professors, administrators, and peers (Allen 1992; Hughes 1987; Oliver, Smith, and Wilson 1989; Sedlacek 1987; Davis 1994). The aim of this literature review is to examine the latter of the two factors that affect African American male performance at PWIs.

Numerous studies have analyzed the experiences of Black students attending predominately Black and White institutions. Research has revealed that students on predominately White campuses report that racial discrimination occurs with great frequency (Allen 1992; Davis 1994). While several studies note that some African American students are doing well academically at PWIs, they also report a substantial decrease in these students' performances that surpasses the typical decrease that is expected of students as they adjust to college-level work (Allen 1988; Davis 1994). Although a majority of the available research does not disaggregate the data to be gender specific, it is assumed that Black men are duly impacted by previous findings. Furthermore, recent statistics indicate that only 40 percent of Black students who begin college will ultimately graduate compared with more than 61 percent of White students (Cross and Slater 2004; Guiffrida and Douthit 2010). Additionally, Bowen and Bok (1998) found the class ranks of Black students at PWIs to be lower than those of White students at PWIs even after controlling for variables such as Scholastic Assessment Test (SAT) scores, high school GPA, socioeconomic status, gender, selectivity of schools, and fields of study. At almost every selective college in their sample, racial or ethnic minority students' academic performances were below that of White students' and at levels lower than what was predicted by their SAT scores. Additionally, Black students who graduate from PWIs tend to have substantially lower grade point averages (GPAs) than do the predominant group (Bowen and Bok 1998; Guiffrida and Douthit 2010). This research strongly supports the conception that Black students, inclusive of Black males, encounter noncognitive barriers that affect their chances to succeed at college (Guiffrida and Douthit 2010).

Research on the experiences of African American students in higher education has concentrated primarily on two areas: (1) the differential experience of these students relative to White students and (2) the differential effects of attending a predominately White institution as opposed to a historically Black one (Bowen and Bok 1998; Guiffrida and Douthit 2010). Very little work has focused on the variations in gender experiences as it relates to racism at PWIs for African American students. The existing research generally focuses on the declining participation and increased attrition rates of African American males in higher education (Green and Wright 1992; Davis 1994), while paying little attention to the qualitative aspects of these students' schooling experiences as they relate to racism.

Increased experiences of racism demand that an individual implement coping strategies to deal with the environmental stressor(s). Which coping responses an individual uses (adaptive and/or maladaptive) in turn influences mental health outcomes (Szymanski and Obiri 2011). Other research has theorized that racial discrimination may lead to the use of more maladaptive coping strategies, which in turn may lead to poorer psychosocial and physical health. Diaz (1998) posited that experiences of racial discrimination limit an individual's ability to behave as an active agent in shaping her or his own life, which often leads to feelings of powerlessness, impotence, disillusionment, and confusion and results in increased use of passive or maladaptive coping strategies.

My purpose in this article is primarily to provide an examination of the current literature and to note previous studies that highlight African American males' experiences with racism. I will first provide a brief overview of the experiences of African Americans, specifically African American males, at predominately White campuses. Next, I will briefly discuss racism and how it is defined for the purpose of this examination.

This will provide the background to the primary purpose, which is to explore the biopsychosocial effects and maladaptive coping strategies that are employed when African American males encounter racism-related events. Finally, I will discuss the current literature and propose ideals for future research.

It is important to note that this examination of the literature represents a portion of a larger study that has been designed to understand some of the race-related issues that African American males face as students at PWIs and seeks strategies to address these issues. African American male students were the focus of this examination because this subpopulation of college students brings unique developmental issues and challenges to PWIs (Singer 2005; Smith, Allen, and Danley 2007; Smith, Hung, and Franklin 2011). African American males carry the burden of being students in a Eurocentric educational system (Singer 2005), and, as students in a predominately White environment, they must cope with the stresses of racism, prejudice, and race-related discrimination.

Background

Because it affects educational performance and the quality of the student's overall educational experience, the perceived campus racial climate is a critical factor (Allen 1988, 1992; Altback and Lomotey 1991; Hughes 1987; Nettles 1988; Oliver, Smith, and Wilson 1989; Sedlacek 1987; Cureton 2003). Research has found that African American males may encounter a "culture shock" when they arrive on the campus of PWIs, therefore resulting in social adaptation problems (Brown 2001; Cureton 2003). Problems adapting to a new, predominately White environment and culture could possibly function as an academic progress deterrent because Black students may be more likely than White students to express negative feelings or attitudes toward the university environment (Cureton 2003). Research has also indicated that African American students must make significant personal, family, and social adjustments to attend predominantly White institutions, especially if the campus is not in close proximity of home. Many come from communities and high schools in which they were in the majority; however, when transitioning to PWIs they are confronted with prejudice and racism from students, faculty, and administrators (D'Augelli and Hershberger 1993).

D'Augelli and Hershberger (1993) conducted research on African American student experiences at PWIs and found only 11 percent of the African American students in the sample reported never having heard disparaging remarks about Blacks on campus; 41 percent reported hearing such remarks occasionally, 28 percent heard them often, and 20 percent heard them frequently. Researchers also found that a sample of African American student experiences on campus was related to lower wellbeing (Bridges 2010). Conversely, some African American students had developed important support systems for themselves and these networks served to help prevent discriminatory events from having a psychological impact to the extent they "would jeopardize a student's class attendance and studying" (D'Augelli and Hershberger 1993, 70). However, not all African American students may have adapted positive coping strategies such as these to deal with the implications of racism and prejudice. Numerous reports of racism and cultural insensitivity on many college campuses suggest that these exclusive campus communities are not as cohesive as they appear (Haralson 1995).

In order for Black students to feel a sense of belonging at PWIs, Tinto (1993) has theorized that it is especially important for Black students to become socially integrated into the life of the university to succeed (Guiffrida and Douthit 2010). One way that they can become integrated with the social climate of the campus is to build significant relationships with faculty. Faculty-student relationships are strongly positively correlated with student satisfaction with college (Astin 1999; Guiffrida and Douthit 2010). Although researchers suggest relationships with faculty are especially important to the success of racial and ethnic minority students (Braddock 1981), studies indicate that Black students are often unable to form strong relationships with White faculty at PWIs (Fleming 1984; Mayo, Murguia, and Padilla 1995; Schwitzer, Griffen, Ancis, and Thomas 1999; Guiffrida and Douthit 2010).

One reason for the failure of Black students to connect with White faculty is that Black students often perceive White faculty as culturally insensitive. Examples of cultural insensitivity on the part of White faculty include making stereotypical comments about Blacks, generalizing students' opinions in class as representing those of all Blacks, and failing to acknowledge and incorporate Black perspectives into their curricula (Fries-Britt and Turner 2002; Guiffrida 2005a; Guiffrida and Douthit 2010). Moreover, African American males may be experiencing the residual effects of slavery and an inability to form positive self-identities and their academic performances may be linked inextricably to teacher biases and or the cultural dispositions of others (Douglas 2007; Bell 2010). As a result, these negatively held beliefs of the dominant culture may have hindered the academic aptitude of African American males (Douglass 2007; Bell 2010).

Research conducted in 1972 found that Black students expected more social acceptance than they received at PWIs, therefore resulting in feelings of anger and despair that contributed to a desire to socially and culturally segregate themselves from White students (Haralson 1995). The need to be socially accepted in some theoretical frameworks is considered a psychological sociocultural stressor (Haralson 1995). One transactional model regards experiences of racism and discrimination on campus as psychological sociocultural stressors. Like other stressors, experiences of prejudice and discrimination are associated with psychological distress that can lead to the maladjustment of students at their respective institutions (Cabrera, Nora, Terenzini, Pascarella, and Hagedorn 1999). Unlike stressors, however, experiences of discrimination are considered unique in that they "(a) are present only among minority students and (b) heighten the feeling of not belonging at the institution with spillover effect on a student's academic performance" (Cabrera et al. 1999, 135).

It has been proven that when members of a minority group encounter low acceptance of their values and culture, they are more likely to perceive this intolerance as a form of discrimination. This intolerance establishes a climate of racial prejudice and discrimination that resonates within the interactions of minority students throughout the campus, thus resulting in "low involvement with different campus communities, that impinges on the minority's student cognitive and affective development as well as his or her decisions to persist in college" (Cabrera et al. 1999, 136). Additionally, in a study conducted by Cabrera et al. (1999) found that social experiences of African American students were negatively dominated by perceptions of discrimination.

Theoretical Framework

Because issues of race and racism are a central focus of this review of literature, a methodological approach capable of capturing how race functions is imperative. Consequently, the review draws upon a critical race methodology grounded in the central tenets of Critical Race Theory (CRT) (Parker 1998). CRT has been characterized by "its insistence on placing race at the center of analysis regarding how whites and their dominant institutions tend to control, assume 'normative standards of whiteness' which result in the ignoring of, and subjugation of, marginalized racial groups" (Parker 1998, 45). Further, CRT broadly describes and theorizes about the "individual, institutional, and societal causes that maintain racial minorities' relative subordination in a post–Civil Rights

American culture" (Jay 2009, 673). Consequently, a critical race methodology affirms the experiences of people of color with, and responses to, racism and other forms of oppression both inside and outside of schools as "valid, appropriate, and necessary forms of data." Further, Parker (1988) argues for the value of conducting a qualitative inquiry with a crucial race lens, noting that the blending of theory and method enhances our ability to utilize lived experiences as a mechanism for directly confronting predominant notions about race and racism in the context of education.

Social Psychological Process

Social psychologists would describe the above mentioned phenomenon as a form of prejudice. Prejudice as defined by Aronson (2008, 303) is a "hostile or negative attitude toward a distinguishable group on the basis of generalizations derived from faulty or incomplete information. Aronson further posits that prejudice acts contain a cognitive component (a stereotype of a set of beliefs about a group), an emotional component (dislike of or active hostility toward the group), and a behavioral component (a predisposition to discriminate against the group whenever possible). One example would be when a person holds a prejudice against Asians; it is assumed, that, with a few exceptions, all Asians are rude and distrust Americans. Therefore, the person is then disposed to behave with hostility and bias toward that particular group (Aronson 2008).

This review of literature is grounded in this particular social psychological theoretical framework because groups who encounter prejudice may be more susceptible to realizing negative self-fulfilling prophesies (Aronson 2008). Prejudice that takes place in a school environment often times can be perceived as various forms of racism and lead to negative consequences for the group or group member. Since most people are unaware of the effects of prejudice on the recipients, it is imperative that researchers continue to delve into the negative direct and indirect consequences of prejudice and racism.

Racism

In this review of literature, racism is operationally defined as beliefs, attitudes, institutional arrangements, and acts that tend to denigrate individuals or groups because of phenotypic characteristics or ethnic group affiliation (Clark, Anderson, Clark, and Williams 1999). Although numerous conceptualizations of racism have been used in the literature, they can be placed into two general categories: attitudinal or behavioral (Sigelman and Welch 1991). Attitudinal racism and ethnic prejudice have both been used to represent attitudes and beliefs that denigrate individuals or groups because of phenotypic characteristics or ethnic group affiliation (Yetman 1985). According to Yetman, behavioral racism (ethnic discrimination), in contrast, is "any act of an individual or institution that denies equitable treatment to an individual or a group because of phenotypic characteristics or ethnic group affiliation" (Clark et al. 1999, 805). Another form of racism is referred to as perceived racism. Perceived racism refers to the "subjective experience of prejudice or discrimination; therefore, perceived racism is not limited to those experiences that may objectively be viewed as representing racism" (Clark et al. 1999, 808).

Biopsychosocial Effects of Racism

College is a transitional period when traditional and nontraditional students undergo new experiences and meet new people as well as face opportunities that may cause stress in their lives. Research has found that adolescents and college students face a variety of negative health outcomes including smoking, drinking, experimenting with illegal drugs, suicide ideation, and unhealthy outcome lifestyle habits such as poor diet and lack of sleep (Parker and Flowers 2003). This increase in exposure to perceived stress levels has led to an extension of therapeutic culture not only in the general public, but in college and university campuses nationwide (Parker and Flowers 2003). In recent years, researchers have found that socio-psychological factors such as racism and alienation have contributed to African American student attrition and academic difficulty in college (Aronson, Fried, and Good 2002; D'Augelli and Hershberger 1993; Fleming 1984; Tinto 1975; Parker and Flowers 2003). Furthermore, the stresses related to racism and prejudice could lead to negative health outcomes of African American male students.

Examining the effects of intergroup racism and intragroup racism in African American men is warranted for at least three important reasons. First, if exposure to racism is perceived as stressful, it may have a negative biopsychosocial consequence. Applied to a college context, this exposure can translate into higher levels of stress and lower schooling satisfactions, which could possibly result in withdraw or transfer. Second, differential exposure to coping responses following perceptions of racism may help account for the within group differences in health outcomes among African American men. Third, if exposure to racism is among the factors related to negative health outcomes in African Americans, specific intervention and prevention strategies could be developed and implemented to lessen its harmful impact. Moreover, the combined effects of chronic and acute perceptions of racism have the potential to contribute to psychological and physiological consequences that may be particularly detrimental in African American men (Clark et al. 1999). Therefore, perceived racism as a potential source of stress should be viewed as having both chronic and acute dimensions.

Research has found that the pattern of association between SES and racism among African Americans depends, partly, on what dimension of racism is assessed. For example, research has indicated that the more covert the expression of racism, the more likely that higher SES African Americans report perceiving their environments as more discriminatory because of their tendency to engage in environments where racism is perceived to be nonexistent. Conversely, lower SES African Americans may be more sensitive to overt racism and as a result report more racism with measures that assess more overt expressions of racism (Clark et al. 1999).

Fernander (2004) suggested that the social realities of discrimination, negative representation in the media, and racism appear to impact Black males more than Black females and this might be a significant factor for explaining negative health outcomes. Additionally, he posited that there remains an assumption that as a Black male's social status increases, the more of a perceived threat he presents to those within the majority. Lastly, agreeing with previously cited research, the higher a Black man's education level, the "more detrimental the psychological or physical health consequences are as a result of how active coping strategies, adaptive or maladaptive, are used to respond to racism-related events" (Smith et al. 2011, 76).

Coping Strategies

Black students were most likely to leave college because of serious adjustment difficulties during the transition from a familiar way of life to an unfamiliar environment (Haralson 1995). "A major barrier to black student retention is the perception by black students that they are outsiders in the academic world, aliens in a hostile environment" (Gibbs 1988, 353). Gibbs (1988) identified withdrawal as the most common adaptation response that Black students employed in coping with identity conflicts associated with White educational environments. Withdrawal can be defined as the desire to avoid contact with conflict producing situations (Gibbs 1988). The second most common coping adaptation was described by Gibbs as separation that was characterized by anger, hostility, and contempt for White middle-class values and behavior patterns (Gibbs 1988; Haralson 1995).

Even among African Americans who perceive certain stimuli as stressful, whether racially based or not, it is important to note that there are a wide variety of individual differences in psychological and physiological stress responses. For example, Lasarus and Folkman (1984) noted that it is both the individual's evaluation of the seriousness of an event and his or her coping responses that determine whether a psychological stress response will ensue (Clark et al. 1999). Coping responses that do not assuage stress responses are considered maladaptive and may negatively affect health (Clark et al. 1999). That is, when maladaptive coping responses are used, the perception of an environmental event as racist will trigger psychological and physiological stress responses. If an individual fails to replace these maladaptive coping responses with more adaptive ones, this model further predicts a continued state of heightened psychological and physiological activity (Selye 1976).

Numerous psychological stress responses may follow perceptions of racism. These responses include anger, paranoia, anxiety, helplessness, hopelessness, frustration, resentment, and fear (Clark et al. 1999). Psychological stress responses may, in turn, influence the use of subsequent coping responses. For example, perceptions of racism may lead the group member to become angered thus resulting in the use of coping responses that include suppression, hostility, aggression, and verbal expression of the anger or the use of alcohol or other substances (Clark et al. 1999). Moreover, chronic feelings of helplessness or hopelessness may evoke feelings of frustration, depression, resentment, distrust, or paranoia that lead to passivity, overeating, avoidance, or efforts to gain control (Clark et al. 1999). These chronic feelings could also ultimately lead to the decreased wellness and educational attainment of African American males at PWIs.

Conclusion

Psychological and physiological responses to racism may, over time, be related to numerous health outcomes. For example, research has found that as a potential added stressor for many African Americans, perceived racism may influence the origin of depression by (a) posing transient threats to self-esteem, (b) making the group's failure to receive normative returns more salient, and (c) contributing to a sense of helplessness (Fernando 1984). Racism-specific coping responses refer to cognitions and behaviors used to mitigate the effect of perceived racism. Although numerous investigators have examined the relationship between general coping responses and health outcomes, few have sought to identify specific coping responses African American males use in response to racism.

Because African American males may use negative coping strategies to combat the stress of racism, this literature review aims to examine the potential effects of using negative coping strategies as applied in the higher education environment. Furthermore, African American students at PWIs may need additional intervention to address issues of racial discrimination, isolation, and coping, as well as other factors common to all students at PWIs, such as control and self-esteem. In summary, ongoing research that explores the implications of racism, as it relates to African American males, is absolutely necessary to their educational attainment at predominately White institutions.

References

Abraham, A. A., and Southern Regional Educational Board. *Racial Issues on Campus: How Students View Them.* Southern Regional Education Board, 1990.

Allen, Walter R. "Black Student, White Campus: Structural, Interpersonal, and Psychological Correlates of Success." *Journal of Negro Education* 54, no. 2 (1985): 134–47.

———. *Gender and Campus Race Differences in Black Student Academic Performance, Racial Attitudes and College Satisfaction.* Atlanta, GA: The Southern Education Foundation, 1986.

———. "The Color of Success: African-American College Student Outcomes at Predominantly White and Historically Black Public Colleges and Universities." *Harvard Educational Review* 62, no. 1 (1992): 26–44.

Allen, W. R., E. Epps, and N. Haniff, eds. *College in Black and White: African American Students in Predominantly White and in Historically Black Public Universities.* Albany, NY: State University of New York Press, 1991.

Amirkhan, J. H. "A Factor Analytically Derived Measure of Coping: The Coping Strategy Indicator." *Journal of Personality and Social Psychology,* 59, no. 5 (1990): 1066–1074.

Anthony, T. D., W. A. Kritsonis, and D. E. Herrington. National Cry for Help: Psychological Issues as They Relate to Education; A Realistic Approach to Understanding and Coping with the African American Males. Lamar University Electronic Journal of Student Research (2007).

Aronson, E. *The Social Animal.* New York: Worth Publishers, 2008.

Aronson, J., C. B. Fried, and C. Good. "Reducing the Effects of Stereotype Threat on African American College Student by Shaping Theories of Intelligence." *Journal of Experimental Social Psychology* 38, no. 2 (2002): 113–125.

Astin, A.W. "How the Liberal Arts College Affects Students." *Distinctively American: The Residential Liberal Arts Colleges* 128 (1999): 77–100.

Astin, H. S. and P. H. Cross. *Characteristics of Entering Black Freshmen in Predominately Black and Predominately White Institutions: A Normative Report.* Rhode Island: Higher Education, 1977.

Bacon, E., J. Banks, K. Young, and F. R. Jackson. "Perceptions of African American and European American Teachers on the Education of African American Boys." *Multiple Voices for Ethnically Diverse Exceptional Learners* 10, no. 1–2 (2007): 160–172.

Beckham, B. "Strangers in a Strange Land: The Experience of Blacks on White Campuses." *Educational Record* 6869, no. 41 (1998): 74–78.

Bell, E. E. "Educating African American Males." Online Submission, 2010.

———. "Understanding African American Males." Online Submission, 2010.

Bowen, W. G. and D. Bok. *The Shape of the River: Long-Term Consequences of Considering Race in College and University Admission.* Princeton, NJ: Princeton University Press, 1988.

Braddock, J. H. "Race, Athletics, and Educational Attainment: Dispelling the Myths." *Youth and Society* 12, no. 3 (1981): 335–351.

Bridges, E. "Racial Identity Development and Psychological Coping Strategies of African American Males at Predominately White University." *Annals of the American Psychotherapy Association* 13, no, 1 (2010): 14–26.

Britts, M. W. *Blacks on White College Campuses.* 1976.

Brown, T. "Exposure to All Black Contexts and Psychological Well-Being: The Benefits of Racial Concentration." *African American Research Perspectives* 7 (2001): 157–172.

Buncombe, M. H. "Black Students on White Campuses: Damaged Goods." *Critique* 4, no. 4 (1973).

Buser, J. K. "Treatment-Seeking Disparity Between African Americans and Whites: Attitudes toward Treatment, Coping Resources, and Racism." *Journal of Multicultural Counseling and Development* 37, no. 2 (2009): 94.

Byrd, M. L., and A. L. Sims. "Communication Apprehension among Black Students on Predominantly White Campuses." *Western Journal of Black Studies* 11, no. 3 (1987): 105–10.

Cabrera, A. F., A. Nora, P. T. Terenzini, E. Pascarella, and L. S. Hagedorn. "Campus Racial Climate and the Adjustment of Students to College: A Comparison between White Students and African-American Students." *Journal of Higher Education* 70, no. 2 (1999): 134–60.

Canillas, G. J. *African American Men: Psychotherapeutic Process as a Coping Style.* 1992.

Clark, M., and Others. "Dating Preferences and Patterns of Black Students on Predominantly White Campuses." (1983).

Clark, R. "Interethnic Group and Intraethnic Group Racism: Perceptions and Coping in Black University Students." *Journal of Black Psychology* 30, no. 4 (2004): 506–526.

Clark, R., N. B. Anderson, V. R. Clark, and D. R. Williams. "Racism as a Stressor for African Americans: A Biopsychosocial Model." *American Psychologist* 54, no. 10 (1999): 805–16.

Closson, R. B. "Critical Race Theory and Adult Education." *Adult Education Quarterly* 60, no. 3 (2010): 261–283.

Cole, E. R. and K. R. J. Arriola. "Black Students on White Campuses: Toward a Two-Dimensional Model of Black Acculturation." *Journal of Black Psychology* 33, no. 4 (2007): 379–403.

Cross, T. and R. B. Slater. "The Financial Footing of the Black Colleges." *The Journal of Blacks in Higher Education* 6 (1994): 76–79.

Cureton, S. R. "Race-Specific College Student Experiences on a Predominantly White Campus. *Journal of Black Studies* 33, no. 3 (2003): 295–311.

Dancy II, Theodis E. "Madness or Elitism? African Americans Who Reject HBCUs." *Black Issues in Higher Education* 22, no. 5 (2005): 82.

D'Augelli, A. R. and S. L. Hershberger. "African American Undergraduates on a Predominantly White Campus: Academic Factors, Social Networks, and Campus Climate." *Journal of Negro Education* 62, no. 1 (1993): 67–81.

Davis, J. E. "College in Black and White: Campus Environment and Academic Achievement of African American Males." *Journal of Negro Education* 63, no. 4 (1994): 620–33.

Davis, R. D. "Safe Havens for African American Students: Finding Support on a White Campus." draft. (1994).

De Walt, P. S. *First Generation U.S.-Born Africans and the Expanded Nigrescence Theory: The Stretching of a Theory for a "Different" African American Experience at a Predominantly White Institution of Higher Education.* Ann Arbor, MI: ProQuest, 2009.

Diaz, E. "Perceived Factors Influencing the Academic Underachievement of Talented Students of Puerto Rican Descent." *The Gifted Child Quarterly* 42, no. 2 (1998): 105.

Faison, J. J. "The Next Generation: The Mentoring of African American Graduate Students on Predominately White University Campuses." Paper presented at the annual meeting of the American Educational Research Association, New York, NY, April 8–12, 1996.

Feagin, J. R. and M. P. Sikes. "How Black Students Cope With Racism on White Campuses." *Journal of Blacks in Higher Education* 8 (1995): 91–97.

Fisher, D. "Creating a Schoolwide Vocabulary Initiative in an Urban High School." *Journal of Education for Students Placed at Risk* 12, no. 3 (2007).

Fleming, J. *Blacks in College: A Comparative Study of Students' Success in Black and in White Institutions.* San Francisco: Jossey-Bass Higher Education Series, 1990.

Flowers, L. A. "Effects of College Racial Composition on African American Students' Interactions with Faculty." *College Student Affairs Journal* 23, no. 1 (2003): 54–63.

Fries-Britt, S. and B. Turner. "Facing Stereotypes: A Case Study of Black Students on a White Campus." *Journal of College Student Development* 42, no. 5 (2001): 420–29.

Gibbs, J. T. "Black Students/White University: Different Expectations." *Personnel and Guidance Journal* 51, no. 7 (1988): 436–469.

Green, R. L. and D. L. Wright. "African-American Males: A Demographic Study and Analysis." in *A Discussion of Issues Affecting African-American Men and Boys,* edited by B. W. Austin, 27–78. Battle Creek, MI: W. K. Kellogg Foundation, 1992.

Gregory, S. T. "Selected Innovations in Higher Education Designed to Enhance the Racial Climate for Students of Color in Predominately White Colleges and Universities." Paper presented at the Annual Meeting of the American Educational Research Association, New Orleans, LA, April 24–28, 2000.

Guiffrida, D. A. "Friends from Home: Asset and Liability to African American Students Attending a Predominantly White Institution." *NASPA Journal* 41, no. 4 (2004): 693–708.

Guiffrida, D. A. and K. Z. Douthit. "The Black Student Experience at Predominantly White Colleges: Implications for School and College Counselors." *Journal of Counseling and Development* 88, no. 3 (2010): 311–318.

Haralson, M. "The Relationship between Assertiveness and the Persistence of Successful Black Male Students in Predominantly White Institutions of Higher Education: A Comprehensive Review Paper." [S.l.]: Distributed by ERIC Clearinghouse (1993).

Haralson, Jr., M. "The Influences of Gender, School Year, and Socioeconomic Status on Assertiveness for Blacks at Predominantly White Universities. Paper presented at Annual Meeting of the Georgia Educational Research Association, Atlanta, GA, October 26, 1995.

———. "Survival Factors for Black Students on Predominantly White Campuses." Paper presented at the Annual Meeting of the National Association of Student Personnel Administrators, Atlanta, GA, March 13–16, 1996.

Hardiman, R. and B. W. Jackson. "Racial Identity Development: Understanding Racial Dynamics in College Classrooms and on Campus." *Directions for Teaching and Learning* 52 (1992): 21–37.

Hargrove, B. H. and S. E. Seay. "School Teacher Perceptions of Barriers That Limit the Participation of African American Males in Public School Gifted Programs." *Journal for the Education of the Gifted* 34, no. 3 (2011): 434–467.

Harper, S. R. "Leading the Way: Inside the Experiences of High-Achieving African-American Male Students." *About Campus* 10, no. 1 (2005): 8–15.

Harris, S. M. and M. T. Nettles. "Racial Differences in Student Experiences and Attitudes." *New Directions for Student Services* 56 (1991): 25–38.

Hefner, D. "Where the Boys Aren't: The Decline of Black Males in Colleges and Universities Has Sociologists and Educators Concerned about the Future of the African American Community." *Black Issues in Higher Education* 21, no. 9 (2004): 70.

Henry, P. N. "Accommodating Black Students on Traditionally White Campuses: Some Considerations." 1978.

Highlen, P. S., D. M. Tom, K. R. Ashton, and K. I. Thompson "Effects of Perceived Racism and Sexism on Psychological Well Being and the Moderating Effects of Identity Development Among African and European American College Students." Poster presented at the Annual Convention of the American Psychological Association, San Francisco, CA, August 14–18, 1998.

Hiraldo, P. "The Role of Critical Race Theory in Higher Education." *The Vermont Connection* 31 (2010): 53–59.

Hughes, M. "Black Students Participation in Higher Education." *Journal of College Student Personnel* 28 (1987): 532–545.

Isom, D. A. "Performance, Resistance, Caring: Racialized Gender Identity in African American Boys." *Urban Review: Issues and Ideas in Public Education* 39, no. 4 (2007): 405–423.

Jay, M. "Race-ing through the School Day: African American Educators' Experiences with Race and Racism in Schools." *International Journal of Qualitative Studies in Education* 22, no. 6 (2009): 671–685.

Kaba, A. J. "Progress of African Americans in Higher Education Attainment: The Widening Gender Gap and Its Current and Future Implications." *Education Policy Analysis Archives* 13, no. 25 (2005).

Keller, J. and Others. "Perceptions of the College Environment and Campus Life: The Black Experience." *Journal of Non-White Concerns in Personnel and Guidance* 10, no. 4 (1982): 126–32.

Kim, S. H. and W. E. Sedlacek. "Gender Differences among Incoming African American Freshmen on Academic and Social Expectations. Research Report #7–94." Paper presented at the Annual Meeting of the American Educational Research Association, San Francisco, CA, April 18–22, 1995.

King, P. M. and Others. "Intellectual Development of Black College Students on a Predominantly White Campus. ASHE Annual Meeting Paper." Paper presented at the Annual Meeting of the Association for the Study of Higher Education, Atlanta, GA, November 2–5, 1989.

Lazarus, R. S. and S. Folkman. *Stress, Appraisal, and Coping*. New York: Springer, 1984.

Liang, C. T. H., A. N. Alvarez, L. P. Juang, and M. X. Liang. "The Role of Coping in the Relationship between Perceived Racism and Racism-Related Stress for Asian Americans: Gender Differences." *Journal of Counseling Psychology* 54, no. 2 2007): 132–141.

Lynn, M., J. N. Bacon, T, L. Totten, Thurman L., Bridges, III, and M. E. Jennings. "Examining Teachers' Beliefs about African American Male Students in a Low-Performing High School in an African American School District." *Teachers College Record* 112, no. 1 (2010): 289–330.

Maina, F., M. Burrell, and B. Hampton. "Coping Strategies for Students of Color in a Predominantly White College: Voices from the Alumni." Online Submission, 2011.

Malone, R. M. and J. A. Malone. "African American Faculty as Part of the Problem or Part of the Solution in the Retention of African American Students on 'White' College Campuses." Paper presented at the Annual National Conference of the National

Association of African American Studies and the National Association of Hispanic and Latino Studies, Houston, TX, February 21–26, 2000.

Mannan, G. and Others. "A Comparison of the Academic Performance of Black and White Freshman Students on an Urban Commuter Campus." *Journal of Negro Education* 55, no. 2 (1986): 155–61.

Mayo, J. R., E. Murguia, and R. V. Padilla. "Social Integration and Academic Performance among Minority University Students." *Journal of College Student Development* 36 (1995): 542–552.

McLure, G. T., A. M. S. Rao, and W. L. Lester . "Comparing Student Perceptions of General Education and Personal Growth Outcomes at HBCU and Non-HBCU Institutions." Paper presented at the Annual Forum of the Association for Institutional Research, Seattle, WA, May 30–June 3, 1999.

Melendez, M. C. "Black Football Players on a Predominantly White College Campus: Psychosocial and Emotional Realities of the Black College Athlete Experience." *Journal of Black Psychology* 34, no. 4 (2008): 423–451.

Midlands, T. C. *Black Experience In Higher Education Grant. Minority Student Success Study.* Columbia, SC: Midlands Technical College, 1992.

Moore, James L., III. "A Qualitative Investigation of African American Males' Career Trajectory in Engineering: Implications for Teachers, School Counselors, and Parents." *Teachers College Record* 108, no. 2 (2006): 246–266

Nasim, A., A. Roberts, J. P. Harrell, and H. Young. "Non-Cognitive Predictors of Academic Achievement for African Americans across Cultural Contexts." *Journal of Negro Education* 74, no. 4 (2005): 344–358.

Negga, F., S. Applewhite, and I. Livingston. "African American College Students and Stress: School Racial Composition, Self-Esteem and Social Support." *College Student Journal* 41, no. 4 (2007): 823–830.

Nelson Laird, T. F., B. K. Bridges, C. Morelon-Quainoo, J. M. Williams, and M. S. Holmes. "African American and Hispanic Student Engagement at Minority Serving and Predominantly White Institutions." *Journal of College Student Development* 48, no. 1 (2007): 39–56.

Nettles, M. T. *Toward Black Undergraduate Student Equality in American Higher Education.* New York: Greenwood Press, 1988.

Obiakor, F. E. and W. R. "African-American Males Experiencing School Failure: Alternative Self-Concept Model for Special Educators." Paper presented at the Council for Exceptional Children's Topical Conference on At-Risk Children and Youth, New Orleans, LA, November 10–12, 1991.

Oliver, M., A. Smith, and K. Wilson. "Supporting Successful Black Students: Personal, Organizational, and Institutional Factors." *National Journal of Sociology* 3 (1989) 199–221.

Palmer, R. T. and E. M. Young. "Determined to Succeed: Salient Factors that Foster Academic Success for Academically Unprepared Black Males at a Black College." *Journal of College Student Retention: Research, Theory and Practice* 10, no. 4 (2009): 465–482

Parker, L. "Race is Race Ain't: An Exploration of the Utility of Critical Race Theory in Qualitative Research in Education." *International Journal of Qualitative Studies in Education* 11, no. 1 (1998): 43–55.

Parker, M. and L. A. Flowers. "The Effects of Racial Identity on Academic Achievement and Perceptions of Campus Connectedness on African American Students at Predominantly White Institutions." *College Student Affairs Journal* 22, no. 2 (2003): 180–94.

Pascarella, T. and P. Terenzini. *How College Affects Students: A Third Decade of Research.* San Francisco: Jossey-Bass, 1991.

Patton, L. D. and C. Catching. "'Teaching While Black': Narratives of African American Student Affairs Faculty." *International Journal of Qualitative Studies in Education* 22, no. 6 (2009): 713–728.

Rodgers, K. A. and J. J. Summers. "African American Students at Predominantly White Institutions: A Motivational and Self-Systems Approach to Understanding Retention." *Educational Psychology Review* 20, no. 2 (2008): 171–190.

Rodgers, R. S. and W. E. Sedlacek. *Racial Attitudes of White University Freshmen by Sex.* College Park, MD: University of Maryland, 1979.

Rosenthal, S. J. "Racism and the Campus Environment: Student Attitudes and Perceptions." Paper presented at the National Conference on Desegregation in Higher Education, Raleigh, NC, July 19, 1979.

Ross, S., B. Niebling, and T. M. Heckert. "Sources of Stress among College Students." *College Student Journal* 33, no. 2 (1999): 312–317.

Schwitzer, A.M., O. T. Griffin, J. R. Ancis, and C. R. Thomas. "Social Adjustment Experiences of African American College Students." *Journal of Counseling and Development* 77, no. 2 (1999): 189–198.

Scott, H. J. "Will Retrenchments Destroy Equal Educational Opportunity?" Paper presented at the Institute for the Study of Afro-American Life and History, Detroit, MI, October 1983.

Sedlacek, W. E. "Black Students on White Campuses: 20 Years of Research." *Journal of College Student Personnel* 28, no. 6 (1987): 484–95.

Seyle, H. "Forty Years of Stress Research: Principal Remaining Problems and Misconceptions." *Canadian Medicine Association Journal* 115, no. 1 (1976): 53–56.

Shorter-Gooden, K. "Multiple Resistance Strategies: How African American Women Cope with Racism and Sexism." *Journal of Black Psychology* 30, no. 3 (2004): 406–425.

Sigelman, L. *Black Americans' Views of Racial Inequality: The Dream Deferred.* New York: Cambridge University Press, 1991.

Singer, J. N. "Understanding Racism through the Eyes of African American Male Student-Athletes." *Race, Ethnicity and Education* 8, no. 4 (2005): 365–386.

Spaights, E., D. Kenner, and H. E. Dixon. "The Relationship of Assertiveness and the Academic Success of Black Students in Predominately White Institutions of Higher Education." *A Journal of Human Behavior* 24, no. 3 (1987): 9–16.

Spratlen, T. H. "The Continuing Factor of Black Economic Inequity in the United States." *Western Journal of Black Studies* 6, no. 2 (1982): 73–79.

Smith, W. A., N. Hung, and J. D. Franklin. "Racial Battle Fatigue and the Miseducation of Black Men: Racial Microaggressions, Societal Problems, and Environmental Stress." *The Journal of Negro Education* 80, no. 1 (2011): 63–82.

Smith, W. A., W. R, Allen, and L. L. Danley. "Psychosocial Experiences and Racial Battle Fatigue among African American Male College Students." *American Behavioral Scientist* 51, no. 4 (2007): 551–578.

Strayhorn, T. L. and M. C. Terrell, eds. *The Evolving Challenges of Black College Students: New Insights for Policy, Practice, and Research.* Sterling, VA: Stylus Publishing, 2010.

Szymanski, D. M. and O. Obiri. "Do Religious Coping Styles Moderate or Mediate the External and Internalized Racism-Distress Links?" *Counseling Psychologist* 39, no. 3 (2011): 438–462.

Taylor, M. C. "Academic Performance of Blacks on White Campuses." *Integrated Education* 16, no. 5 (1978): 28–31.

Terenzini, P. T., P. M. Yaeger, L. Bohr, E. T. Pascarella, and N. Amaury. "African American College Students' Experiences in HBCUs and PWIs and Learning Outcomes." Paper presented at the Annual Meeting of the Association for Institutional Research, Orlando, FL, May 1997.

Thompson, G. L. *Up Where We Belong: Helping African American and Latino Students Rise in School and in Life*. San Francisco: Jossey-Bass, 2007.

Tinto, V. "Dropout from Higher Education: A Theoretical Synthesis of Recent Research." *Review of Educational Research* 45, no. 1 (1975): 89–125.

———. *Leaving College: Rethinking the Causes and Cures of Student Attrition*. Chicago: University of Chicago Press, 1993.

Tracey, T. J. and W. E. Sedlacek. *The Relationship of Noncognitive Variables to Academic Success by Race over Four Years*. College Park, MD: University of Maryland, 1984.

Trevino, F.M. *Health Indicators for Hispanic, Black and White Americans*. Washington, DC: U.S. Dept. of Health and Human Services, 1984.

Utsey, S. O., J. G. Ponterotto, A. L. Reynolds, and A. A. Cancelli. "Racial Discrimination, Coping, Life Satisfaction, and Self-Esteem among African Americans." *Journal of Counseling and Development* 78, no. 1 (2000): 72–80.

Washington, N. C. "Effective Coping Strategies Employed in African-American Relationships." Paper presented at the Annual Convention of the American Psychological Association, Washington, DC, August 14–18, 1992.

Wells-Lawson, M. "The Effects of Race and Type of Institution on the College Experiences of Black and White Undergraduate Students Attending 30 Predominantly Black and Predominantly White Colleges and Universities." Paper presented at the Annual Meeting of the American Educational Research Association, New Orleans, LA, April 4–8, 1994.

Yetman, N. R. *Majority and Minority: The Dynamics of Race and Ethnicity in American Life*. Boston: Allyn and Bacon, 1985.

4

They Fought a Good Fight:
SNCC and Civil Rights in Mississippi

Rochelle Brock

Anybody hada just told me 'fore it happened that conditions would make this change between the white and the black in Holmes County here where I live, why I just wouldn't have believed it. I didn't dream of it. I didn't see no way. But it got to workin' just like the citizenship class teacher told us—that if we would redish to vote and just stick with it. He says it's gon' be some difficults. He told us when we started. We was lookin' for it. He said we gon' have difficults, gone have troubles, folks gon' lose their homes, folks gon' lose their lives, peoples gon' Lose all their money, and just like he said, all of that happened. He didn't miss it. He hit it kap-dap on the head, and it's workin' now. It won't never go back where it was.
—Hartman Turnbow (quoted in Raines 1977)

There was another Negro who one day came to a strange town in Mississippi where he had never been before. When he got off the bus he did not see any of the race around, so he asked a white man, "Where do the colored folks hang out here?"

The white man pointed at a great big tree in the public square and said, "Do you see that limb?"
—Langston Hughes (quoted in Raines 1977, 457–458)

Throughout the twentieth century African American people waged a relentless battle for "freedom" that manifested itself in the fight for voting rights, an end to social injustice, and the struggle for equality and equity in education. During the Civil Rights Movement the struggle took many forms and had different actors, but all involved parties held the common desire of empowering African American people. Members and leaders of the NAACP, SCLC, SNCC, COFO, CORE, and MFDC, although possessing dichotomous ideological and political agendas, nevertheless, held a belief and determination to see African American people enfranchised morally, spiritually, and politically. Despite their dedication to a particular form of action, the various factions fought and sometimes died for their belief in African American human rights. The radical and militant SNCC developed a penchant for "in your face" activism, while the liberal and nonviolent SCLC marched in the long walk to freedom. In contrast to both SCLC and SNCC, a conservative and accommodating NAACP attempted to use the courts as a battleground in their war on injustice. Whatever their means, the various organizations worked diligently to force America to deliver the long promised and continuously denied right of citizenship to African Americans.

The struggle for civil rights occurred in the public and private spheres throughout the South, but it was the prolonged conflict in Mississippi that has come to possess a mystical quality in the mind of America. According to John Dittmer (1995, 424), "In no other southern state was mass protest as extensive and as enduring as in Mississippi." Although diverse Civil Rights organizations played a role in the conflict, and made various degrees of gain in the fight for full citizenship, for a brief time it was SNCC that became the spirit and soul of the Mississippi freedom struggle.

My purpose in writing this article is to analyze the traditions of SNCC and to understand the paradigmatic shift that occurred when SNCC took the forefront in the struggle. I first provide a theoretical framework to understand the realities of life for both White and Black Mississippians. I question why Mississippi proved to be the most recalcitrant state in relinquishing long-held beliefs of Black inferiority and affording human rights to its Black citizens. I then look at the concept of empowerment and how SNCC's philosophy of a personal form of organizing enabled Black Mississippians to fight for their rights. Finally, the last part of the article reviews Julius K. Nyerere's philosophy of an African-centered definition of socialism. I struggle to use Nyerere's conceptualization of liberation for Africans in the context of liberation for Black Mississippians. The Black struggle for freedom has been waged throughout the African Diaspora and as many gains that have been made so have there been setbacks. Was the Mississippi freedom struggle a gain or a setback? How can we tell?

The Citizens' Council: Defining Race and Segregation in Mississippi

When SNCC workers first arrived in Mississippi in the early years of 1960s, they were confronted with a practice of systemic racism and segregation that was thoroughly ingrained in the minds of White Mississippians. The glaring inequality between Black and White people in Mississippi showed a high rate of poverty, infant mortality, poor schools, lynching, unjust laws, and unemployment among Black citizens. In addition, an aura of fear enveloped Black Mississippians in their daily lives and dealings with White people. According to John W. Cell (1982), segregation, or the separation of a race, class, or ethnic group by enforced or voluntary residence in a restricted area, cannot be grounded in social equilibrium. Instead, the edifice of segregation is built on tension and imbalance. The ideology of separation serves to mystify the disparities between races, legitimizing the unnaturalness of one race dominating another. Segregation is able to function through the use of interlocking systems of economic institutions, social practices and customs, laws, and beliefs, which serve as the means for a dominant group to maintain and increase its control over a subordinate group. These systems are interlocking because for segregation to be effective, races must be kept physically, intellectually, and spiritually separate in all areas of life.

A segregated society can only thrive when binary opposites are created and used to justify an ideology of difference. This difference has defined American society since the concept of race was developed. Barbara Fields (1982, 143) asserts that "[r]acism has been America's tragic flaw" and that elsewhere in the world the classes struggled over "power and privilege, over oppression and exploitation, over competing senses of justice and right," but in the United States these issues were secondary to "the overarching theme of race." The pervasive theme of race difference in Mississippi is an ideological construct based on the supposition that certain races of humankind are superior and others are inferior.

If the influence of society on race ideology is ignored, then the word race takes on a superficial meaning. We understand it only in terms of the phenotype of an individual; they are defined only by their physical appearance (Fields 1982). Race becomes reified but without any substance. This is not to say that race is not real. As Fields asserts, race is real because "[a]ll ideologies are real, in that they are the embodiment in thought of real social relations" (151). It is important to remember that the idea of race cannot be understood without understanding the context of the social relations in which it arises. For example, to decipher what took place in Mississippi it is not sufficient to simply look at information regarding racial relations throughout the South. Instead, historical and contemporary social relations of Black and White Mississippians must also be analyzed.

How do we begin the process of deconstructing the ideologies of race and power? Three important concepts in understanding power are the relationships between subject, object, and the Other. As the Other, a person is part of a dichotomous thinking that categorizes people, things, and ideas in terms of their difference from each other—black/white, male/female, reason/emotion, culture/nature. In this way, things gain meaning only in relation to their counterparts. This categorization places one half of the dichotomy as the norm, to which the other half falls beneath in comparison. For a dichotomy to exist, one part of the subject is inherently opposed to its Other. Object and subject are oppositional terms defined by the tensions and struggles they create and are resolved by the subordination of one half of the dichotomy to the other. The tensions and struggles, which exist in dichotomous thinking, influence the tension and imbalance of segregation. Life for Blacks in segregated Mississippi was strife with injustice. The dichotomy between Black and White existence was glaring with Black Mississippians placed at the lowest end of the continuum.

Ideology mystifies dichotomous thinking about race. In either/or binary opposition, feeling retards thought, values obscure facts, and judgment clouds knowledge. In this type of either/or thinking the Other is viewed as an object to be manipulated, controlled, and dominated, which always involves attempts to objectify the subordinate group. We become objects/subjects, dominant/subordinate in relation to each other. As objects, one relinquishes control over one's reality. Instead, one's reality is defined by others, one's identity created by others, and one's history named only in ways that define one's relationship to those who are subject. On the other hand, as subjects, people have the right to define their own reality, establish their own identities, and name their own history.

The power to name the reality of a group is the ultimate form of power over that group. Mississippi was able to maintain its system of domination over Black people because it held the power to name and enforce their lived experience. Through an intricate system of political fascism, segregation, racism, and fear, White Mississippians utilized the notion of Black people as the Other in their effort to maintain power. The main vehicle for preserving domination was Mississippi's Citizens' Council. The brainchild of Robert Patterson, the Citizens' Council was established in Mississippi with the expressed purpose of ensuring segregation and White supremacy through political power. McMillen (1994) states that the Citizens' Council was a reaction to the *Brown* decision and a means of resisting any attempt to carry its tenants to fruition. The Citizens' Council had as its primary task the orchestration of a "regional concert of defiance"

(18) and had members who were "reliable white male citizens organized for the sole purpose of maintaining segregation" (25). According to Tom P. Brady in *Black Monday* (1955), the philosophy of the Citizens' Council called for the nullification of the NAACP, the creation of a forty-ninth state for Negroes, and the abolition of public schools.

Robert Patterson, a hardline segregationist, attracted members to his group in Mississippi by playing on their fear of Black people as the Other. In a leaflet designed by Patterson, the Citizens' Council stated that they could prove that "crime, illegitimacy, and venereal disease were more prevalent among Negroes than among whites and that, according to the 'frank statement' of a South Carolina NAACP official, intermarriage invari-ably followed integration" (McMillen 1995, 35) The fear and animosity toward Black people most often took on a sexual connotation. Black men were often lynched and their private body parts mutilated because of a fallacious report that an impropriety had been "committed" toward a White woman. The fear of intermarriage, miscegenation, and mongrelization were used to rile White citizens in the cause against integration.

In addition to the leaflet, Patterson also produced a tape recording of a fictitious NAACP member reporting that White women, dissatisfied with White men, held secret cravings for Black men. Patterson went on to say that this proved that "the N.A.A.C.P. and their insolent agitators are little concerned with an education for the 'ignorant nigger'; but, rather, are 'demanding' integration in the white bedroom" (McMillen 1995, 36). In the propaganda released by the newsletter, *The Citizens' Council*, the message was carried that White liberals were "perfidious" and Negroes "diseased, depraved, and crime-prone" (McMillen 1995, 37).

The propaganda of the Citizens' Council was effective because it played on the racial stereotypes of the time. Although Black people had been viewed as a deficient Other since the creation of racial categories, the ideology behind the stereotypes had changed. Black people now had to be viewed as in need of total segregation from decent White people— read White women—so that their lascivious ways could be controlled. Ideologies are not static; they change according to the needs of society. Fields (1982, 154) states that because they consist of "contradictory and inconsistent elements," ideologies "can undergo fundamental change sim-ply through the reshuffling of those elements into a different hierarchy," and even though racialist thinking may not have changed "there was a decisive shift in its character."

Earlier it was stated that the power to name something gives power over what is named. In addition, it was posited that the transformation of the object into the subject means that people have the right to define their own reality, establish their own identity, and name their own history. How do people move from objectification to being subjects in the world? In particular, how did Black Mississippians begin the process of ending their domination and subordination to a White society? The next part of the article answers these questions by looking at SNCC in Mississippi.

Empowering the People

Nobody never come out into the country and talked to real farmers and things . . . because this is the this country has done: it divided us into classes, and if you hadn't arrived at a certain level, you wasn't treated no better by the blacks than you was by the whites. And it was these kids what broke a lot of this down. They treated us like we were special and we loved 'em . . . We didn't feel uneasy about our language might not be right or something. We just felt like we could talk to "em. We trusted 'em, and I can tell the world those kids done their share in Mississippi.
–Fannie Lou Hammer (quoted in Raines 1977, 223)

Although all of the Civil Rights organizations played a role, the young workers of SNCC became the soul of the freedom struggle in Mississippi. It was these individuals who understood that the essence of the Civil Rights Movement *had* to be the empowerment of all African Americans and nowhere was this more evident than in the work of SNCC in Mississippi.

Dittmer (1995) provides three explanations for the character of the Mississippi movement. First, the local people had been fighting for their rights since World War II veterans stood up to Theodore Bilbo in 1946 led by the activism of Megar Evers and Amzie Moore and the "indigenous leadership" of Fannie Lou Hammer. Second, the state produced and attracted young activists because of its reputation. In many of the firsthand accounts from movement activist people tell of wanting to go to Mississippi and fight since they saw and read about the story of Emmett Till. According to Bob Moses, the basis for what happened in the Mississippi movement was due to cadres of approximately two dozen, native Mississippians who committed themselves to the movement full time. Finally, it was SNCC organizers who empowered Black people by making them believe that they could take control of their lives.

In *I've Got the Light of Freedom: The Organizing Tradition and The Mississippi Freedom Struggle* Charles Payne explores the early years of the Mississippi Movement and particularly the relationship between SNCC field organizers and "local people." Payne makes it clear that a symbiotic relationship, which was steeped in mutual respect and need, developed between the young students of SNCC and the residents of Mississippi. By infusing the history of the Mississippi Movement with the day-to-day organizing activities, Payne shows that the success of Mississippi was due to the character, courage, and commitment of the individuals involved. Moreover, Payne illuminates how the ethos of "the personal is political" found its genesis in the Mississippi Movement with successful activism dependent on higher levels of individual trust and meaningful personal relationships between SNCC workers and Black Mississippians. The activism in Mississippi possessed a transformative character because the organizing was personal, thereby fostering a politics of community and interdependence.

Robin Kelly (1995) asserts that in order to understand the political history of an oppressed group you must also understand and refer to infrapolitics. Although Kelly uses this term to explain the everyday resistance of oppressed people to their oppression and the "hidden transcripts" they enact, in the case of the Mississippi freedom struggle, infrapolitics refers to the political relationship between the local people of Mississippi and the students of SNCC. This political alliance helped to construct the social and cultural spaces where Black people were encouraged to express their indigenous knowledge and rights. Similar to Toni Morrison's use of a community of Black women as the "healing force" in her novels, Payne shows that the symbiotic relationship between the community and SNCC, as well as within the community, was an integral part to the success of the Mississippi freedom struggle.

Primarily led by SNCC, Mississippi was a movement of Black people who could finally realize their indigenous empowerment. Empowerment is an often misunderstood and misappropriated concept because words are the perfect mediums through which miscommunication occurs, for they carry with their meanings a set of baggage filled with preconceived notions. The preconception, or emotive sensations, certain words instill in us are based in part on their subjective interpretations. We experience language and that experience gives meaning to the word. In other words, our definition comes from what the word represents and how it fits into our individual ideology. For this purpose, it is necessary to qualify the term as it is used throughout this article.

In Webster's dictionary, *empower* is defined as the ability "to authorize; delegate authority, to enable; permit." According to this definition, empowerment denotes a paternalistic attitude, something doled out by a dominating force. If empowerment is defined and conceptualized according to the definition in Webster's dictionary, then it is paternalistic and a pejorative term. Therefore, when many use empowerment they speak of its "pitfalls" and how it contributes to disvaluing the traditional and vernacular forms of power. As it turns out, what empowerment has actually accomplished is to persuade people that real power can only be theirs if they acquiesce and become part of the dominant paradigm.

For example, James Moore stated that he believed that Medgar Evers was a better leader of the NAACP then his brother, Charles Evers, because he trusted in the intelligence and wants of the people. On the other hand, Charles was "always trying to interfere in the operations of the local branch (of the NAACP) and always uncomfortable with its militance" (Payne 1995, 319). Charles Evers and the NAACP in general believed in the dominant paradigm of American ideology and felt that working within the system on a nonconfrontational manner was the best strategy. Empowerment of Black people, especially poor Blacks in Mississippi, was paternalistic in that the middle-class members of the NAACP did not truly believe these people could effectively operate on their own. According to Fannie Lou Hammer, America had "divided Black people into classes, and if you hadn't arrived at a certain level, you wasn't treated no better by the blacks than you was by the whites" (Raines 1977, 233). The failure of the NAACP in Mississippi was partially due to a class division between the elite NAACP members and the masses of poor Black Mississippians. Just as in the White community, many Black elites felt superior to and responsible for the uplift of their downtrodden brother.

In contrast to the paternalistic definition of empowerment that the NAACP held, SNCC saw empowering Black people as providing them the knowledge people need to possess so as not to acquiesce. SNCC realized that people's indigenous power was the large and small forms of resistance and change people practiced in their daily lives. According to Robin Kelly (1993), in the past Black people practiced small forms of resistance by engaging in activities such as dressing up to go out on Saturday night or wearing Zoot suits. Although seemingly insignificant, these acts represented resistance on two levels. First, dressing up and going out on the town was a normal, typical occurrence for most people, but for African Americans this meant opposing the frustrations and defini- tions White America placed on Blacks. It was a way of saying, "You will not let me live out my humanity in your world, but I can create my own sense of control in my world." Second, Black people engaged in these small forms of resistance not only showed opposition to the system but courage since any form of resistance could result in varying degrees of retaliation from White people. Although seemingly small and unimportant to the insensitive observer, taken in context, the daily acts of resistance exhibited by Black people were just as courageous and necessary as large boycotts or rebellions.

Paramount to a nonpaternalistic concept of empowerment is education. If you talk a farmer into putting his life on the line and registering to vote but do not explain the political process to that farmer, then you have not empowered that person. The men and women in SNCC knew that empowerment was more than voter registration. More importantly, Black people needed to understand the political process, the local and national power the vote can bring, and their rights and responsibilities as citizens. It was for this reason that SNCC held citizenship classes throughout the time of their activism.

Empowerment is a concept rooted in the reality of the person or group seeking empowerment. For Black Mississippians empowerment meant recognizing the insidious ways they were controlled by an ideology of subtle subjugation. To be empowered denotes a consciousness of not only objectification as the Other but also the hegemonic control of a dominant society and what people must do to break that control. For Black Mississippians this meant understanding that they were members of a society that was antithetical to their survival and, therefore, of paramount necessity to their survival was a need for struggle.

To be empowered is to recreate the definition of the Other. To be empowered is to understand how dichotomous thinking works and that it does not have to define who you are. Empowerment is control and agency—not over others, but over self. When Black people are disempowered in society the results are not only failure but also death. This death is both spiritual and physical for when the mind and spirit are not allowed to grow and develop the skill needed to survive in this society, physical death is not far behind.

Through grassroots organizing SNCC developed a strategy of educating Black Mississippians about their objectification and how they held the power to change their own lives. According to Hartman Turnbow, Black Mississippians did not allow themselves to imagine a different world (Rains 1977). The gift SNCC gave to Black residents of Mississippi was the freedom to dream a different and better tomorrow. Dreams are hard to visualize for a dispossessed people, and SNCC recognized that the freedom to envision would only begin when the dispossessed began to take possession of a sense of empowerment.

A nonpaternalistic concept of empowerment means appreciating the knowledge a person already possesses and providing the tools so that previously unused wisdom can become pragmatic. Many of the activists of the 1940s and 1950s were working-class intellectuals, and in the 1960s SNCC's strength came from their ability to tap into these resources (Bond 2000; Payne 1995). For example, although the NAACP ignored Robert Burns—possibly because of his third-grade education—he became a source of invaluable assistance to the workers of SNCC. According to Burns, SNCC had the power to make a difference and afforded him the vehicle to put into action all that he had been thinking about for years. He states, "[B]ut I always had this in mind with anything, anything set up by man can be torn down by man"(quoted in Payne 1995, 183). He goes on to explain that although he knew something could be done about the unjust treatment of Black Mississippians he could not do it alone.

The workers of SNCC understood the knowledge that could be gained from their elders. From Robert Burns to Aaron Henry, the older generation held an intimate knowledge of the "ways of white folk" that the younger generation did not possess. Patricia Hill Collins (1990) calls it the "outsider within" perspective of a generation of Black people who came into contact with White America through informal and formal working relations. Hill-Collins posits that this perspective allowed the material backdrop for a unique view of the "contradictions between the dominant group's actions and ideologies" (11). The intimate knowledge of White people that Burns and Henry provided fostered the development of strategies to fight the oppression. The age-old adage "Know thy enemy" was built on truth; it is difficult to fight what you cannot see.

SNCC was able to channel the activism and knowledge of both young and old Black Mississippians into a machine that fought for the full entry of Black people into the rights of citizenship. Confronted with antagonistic law enforcement, the powers of the Citizens' Council, benign neglect from the federal government, attempts at intimidation from the Ku Klux Klan, and a White society not willing to part with its air of superiority, these folks nevertheless persevered. Gains were made in political representation, economics, school desegregation, and equal treatment under the law. Perhaps the greatest and most fulfilling gain was the sense of self that the movement gave to Black Mississippians. For many Black people the realization of their objectification and how to take back control allowed the freedom struggle to continue after the last SNCC worker left Mississippi.

The End

In *Freedom and Socialism: A Selection From Writings and Speeches, 1965–1967* Tanzanian ex-president Julius K. Nyerere stated that he choose the word *Ujamaa* to denote the form of socialism Tanzania desired because it is an African word for what Africans have decided they need for themselves. The second reason Nyerere gives for the appropriateness of Ujamaa is that its literal translation, family-hood, is a foundation of socialism in Tanzania.

The family was important to the success of the movement in Mississippi. Many of the more activist-minded young people were the children of families with involvement in various forms of social defiance. The children of Mrs. McGhee fought and stood up for their rights with or without the assistance of SNCC (Payne 1995, 208–211). When the Quin home was bombed and young children were threatened, Black people in McComb came out in full force to defend themselves (Dittmer 1995). It was a family of community members.

Family in Mississippi meant a family of Black people who were related by the common bond of oppression. Like most families, not all members were actively involved and not all members even cared to be involved. But, also like most families, all received the benefits worked for by some. The infrapolitcs of the community represented self-determination of Black people in determining their own destiny and not having it determined by outside forces.

Nyerere succinctly delineates the dimensions of a socialist society that are necessary for the liberation of an oppressed people. First and foremost, man is the purpose of all social activity in a socialist society. Regardless of a person's achieved or acquired attributes they are considered equal in a socialist society. According to Nyerere, such a system uses the inequalities of man to serve the equality of man. This is socialism according to most that believe in its ideals, and, as Nyerere asserts, it is also part of traditional African society.

Unfortunately, in societies where racism exists the equality of man is not believed in or practiced. George Fredrickson (1996) posits that there is a similarity in the arguments between White supremacists in America and those in South Africa who believe that Blacks are intellectually inferior; incapable of self-government; and unfit to vote, hold office, and associate on an equal basis with Whites. This fact is evident in both America and in Africa where the systems of apartheid and Jim Crow were used to oppress Blacks. Both of these systems could have only taken place where total political disenfranchisement of Blacks occurred. According to Nkrumah, colonialism occurs when the colonial power cements its colonies to itself through political ties (Fredrickson 1996). In Mississippi Blacks were believed to be unequal and incapable of effective self-government so political power was withheld, securing their dependence on those who were in control.

The political power to self-govern or, in the case of American Blacks, to become part of the political system is another part of Nyerere's definition of socialism. Not only must a people's equality be reflected in their political organizations, their representatives must possess the power to make rules and laws that are beneficial to the people. When SNCC first began its work in Mississippi, laws were not beneficial to Black people. Economic intimidation and reprisals were able to control Black people because they were politically powerless to protest or change unfair laws and racist lawmakers.

With political power the tools of production and the mechanism of exchange are under the control of the people. Nkrumah asserts that colonies are useful in that they provide access to raw materials, are a market to sell manufactured goods from the home country, and are a field for investment of surplus capital. He goes on to say that capitalism in colonies happens not by establishing industry, which would lead to competitions with the industries of the home country, but by exhausting the natural and mineral resources of the colonies (Fredrickson 1996). In the economically depressed areas of the Mississippi Delta during the 1960s few Black people were able to own the means of production. Because of systems like sharecropping, not only did they not own the land, they did not even own the human capital of their labor. Throughout Mississippi, violence ensured that many Black people would relinquish their ownership rights of their labor and land to White people.

W.E.B. Du Bois asked that imperialism not be allowed to sacrifice the African to greed for Africa's gold. In America the question was asked for America not to let Mississippi sacrifice its Black citizens to greed or racism. We know that the African and his way of life were sacrificed because a few wanted her precious resources. What were the precious resources of Mississippi that Black people were sacrificed for? Segregation, domination, subordination, White supremacy?

Another point Nyerere makes regarding Ujamaa is that there should be no exploitation of one man by another, and individual freedom should occur where the laws of society are known and applied equally to all people. The exploitation that Nyerere spoke of in the 1960s, Du Bois spoke of in 1900. He requested that the world not continue to refuse the pursuit of happiness to a "striving human soul" and that color not be the determining factor of a person's worth. The racialist attitudes of Mississippi made color the most important thing about a person. Only when you were White, but sympathetic to the Black cause, did color stop being an issue. Dave Dennis of SNCC tells a story of seeing a young woman at the law library of the University of Michigan who he recognized from the Mississippi Movement. This woman was White and a survivor of an incident with the Natchez police. "They held a pistol to her head and played Russian roulette" (quoted in Raines 1977, 273). The job this woman had at the library was part of her therapy at the mental institution she entered after leaving Natchez. Eleven years later she was still in the mental institution. In Mississippi hate and fear were so strong regarding White feelings toward Black people that insane actions became the norm.

What will it take for there to exist the type of society both Du Bois and Nyerere hoped for and SNCC worked to achieve? SNCC put forth a valiant effort to make it happen. Fannie Lou Hammer, Dorie Ladner, Mrs. McGhee, Amzie Moore, and countless others tried to make it work. For a brief time Mississippi was accomplishing the type of liberating socialism Nyerere spoke of. But it ended or was stopped before it could materialize. The Black freedom struggle continues today in different arenas than the struggle of the 1960s. What has remained the same in the struggle from the past and physical enslavement to the present and mental enslavement is that the struggle for liberation and its eventual attainment will take place with the masses. SNCC realized this one fact fifty years ago. For any movement that seeks to liberate a people to be successful it must necessarily began and end with the people.

As a teacher educator and specifically one who works in urban education and with minority school districts I see a significant lesson educators can and should learn from SNCC's work in Mississippi. Some who work in urban education attempt to do so through a paternalistic lens. I call it the "we know what is best for you" syndrome. I have had students believe that they are the savior to the poor Black and Brown K–12 students they will soon be in charge of teaching. They mistakenly view poor and minority students as the cause and reason for the problems they face. I work to rid my students of the their belief in the cultural deficit model or the view that minority students fail to learn as well as other students because their cultures are educationally inadequate and fail to prepare them for good academic performance. Instead, we look at and talk about the various systemic and structural obstacles that impede the success of students.

What can educators learn from SNCC's grassroots organizing? First, SNCC understood the importance of educating Black Mississippians about their objectification and of providing the means to agency. This—to me—is one of the most important lessons I can instill in my students. Rather than just teaching them how to create a lesson plan, take attendance, or any of the other mundane tasks teachers are responsible for, I instruct them on the forms of oppression and, importantly, we discuss the various obstacles that students are faced with. It is important for future teachers to understand the various reasons behind and the possible outcomes of students living in a segregated and unequal society. My teachers in training must also understand how racism affects the lives of the minority—Black and Brown—students they are working with. Ultimately, they must empower themselves and their students to make a positive change in their world. If I can teach my students to have even a little of the courage that the SNCC workers had in Mississippi I feel like I have accomplished something great, and just maybe the students they teach will become the twenty-first-century SNCC workers fighting for justice and a better tomorrow.

References

Brady, T. P. *Black Monday.* Winona, MS: Association of Citizens' Councils, 1955.

Bond, J. "SNCC: What We Did." *Monthly Review* 52, no. 5 (2000) http://monthlyreview.org/2000/10/01/sncc-what-we-did.

Cell, J. W. *The Highest Stage of White Supremacy.* New York: Cambridge University Press, 1982.

De Santis, C., ed. "Jokes Negroes Tell on Themselves." In *The Collected Works of Langston Hughes, vol. 9: Essays on Art, Race, Politics, and World Affairs.* Columbia, MO: University of Missouri Press, 2002.

Dittmer, J. *Local People: The Struggle for Civil Rights in Mississippi.* Chicago: University of Illinois Press, 1995.

Fields, B. "Ideology and Race in American History." *Region, Race, and Reconstruction: Essays in Honor of C. Vann Woodward*, edited by J. Morgan Kousser and James M. McPherson, 143–177. New York: Oxford University Press, 1982.

Fredrickson, G. M. *Black Liberation: A Comparative History of Black Ideologies in the United States and South Africa.* Oxford: Oxford University Press, 1996.

Hill-Collins, P. *Black Feminist Thought: Knowledge, Consciousness, and the Politics of Empowerment.* New York: Routledge, 1990.

Kelly, R. "Black Working-Class Opposition in the Jim Crow South." *The Journal of American History* 80, no. 1 (1993): 75–112.

McMillen, N. R. *The Citizens' Council: Organized Resistance to the Second Reconstruction 1954–64.* Chicago: University of Illinois Press, 1994.

Julius, K. and J. K. Nyerere. *Freedom and Socialism. Uhuru Na Ujamaa; A Selection from Writings and Speeches, 1965–1967.* Oxford: Oxford University Press, 1968.

Payne, C. M. *I've Got the Light of Freedom: The Organizing Tradition and the Mississippi Freedom Struggle.* Berkeley: University of California Press, 1995.

Raines, H. *My Soul Is Rested: The Story of the Civil Rights Movement in the Deep South.* New York: Penguin, 1977.

Ransby, B. "Mentoring a New Generation of Activists: The Birth of the Student Non-violent Coordinating Committee, 1960–1961. In *Ella Baker and the Black Freedom Movement: A Radical Democratic Vision*, edited by B. Ramsby, 239–272. Chapel Hill, NC: University of North Carolina Press, 2003.

Smith, R. S. "Many Minds, One Heart: SNCC's Dream for a New America." *Georgia Historical Quarterly* 94, no. 2 (2010): 244–246.

5

Dayton Funk Music:
The Layering of Multiple Identities[1]

Portia K. Maultsby

"Funk is a Black thing. There is a need to express yourself as an African American.
You need to be your own person."
–Danny Webster, guitarist and vocalist for Slave

This chapter, based on a case study of Dayton Street Funk, employs ethnographic methods combined with the analysis of library and archival sources, recordings, and other artifacts to explore the construction of identities in black popular music. Of central focus are the ways in which identities—manifested in the sonic, lyrical, and visual dimensions of musical performance—juxtapose and superimpose markers of a region, city, *and* local African American communities. The emergence of funk parallels the transition of American society from the era of sanctioned racial segregation known as Jim Crow (1890s–1960s) to the 1970 decade of "integration" and "affirmative action." It also parallels the shift from an industrial to a technological and service-oriented society. Both of these developments helped shape and define the multiple layers of identity associated with funk during its nearly two decades of popularity.

My initial research on Dayton Street Funk was conducted in conjunction with the development of a museum exhibition, "Something in the Water: The Sweet Sound of Dayton Street Funk" for the National Afro-American Museum and Cultural Center (Wilberforce, Ohio), whose objective was to bring greater public and scholarly awareness to this tradition. The approach to this project involved searching for artifacts and memorabilia (musical manuscripts, original recordings, videos of performances, instruments, photographs, album jackets, costumes, posters, promotional materials, etc.), conducting interviews, and locating archival and library materials.[2] The interviews conducted with musicians, high school music teachers, club and retail record store proprietors, radio disc jockeys, parents, local historians, sociologists, and politicians provided a context for interpreting the environment and circumstances that fostered musical creativity throughout Dayton's African American community. These interviews were used in conjunction with local histories of Dayton's African American community, memoirs written by those involved in the funk scene, articles from national and local newspapers as well as music trade publications, analyses of recordings and musical transcriptions and manuscripts, album jackets, photographs, and other memorabilia and artifacts mentioned earlier.

The interpretation of data included the perspectives of musicians and others intimately involved in the creation and popularization of Dayton Street Funk. This collaborative or "double-lens" approach, which former museum curator Rowena Stewart terms "people-oriented" (verses "object-oriented"), combines research methods employed by curators of African American museums with those of ethnomusicologists. Stewart has suggested a five-step approach for collecting and presenting African American documents, one component of which involves the curator enlisting the artifact holders or "keepers of the tradition" in the initial interpretation of the objects, photographs, or documents.[3] Similarly, in the field of ethnomusicology (and other disciplines), participants (e.g., musicians and members of the community) contribute to the interpretation of musical traditions through feedback interviews. This technique involves eliciting comments about a musical performance from the original participants in an attempt to reconstruct its meaning.[4] Current technological media developments in the field of ethnomusicology enable researchers to record and annotate digital video in the field. While viewing the event, participants' comments can be documented using an annotator's program, which allows for a written dialogue about the event.[5]

My approach to this study also considers the social and historical context for the development of funk. Funk, an urban form of dance music, is a byproduct of post–World War II industrial cities, the Vietnam War, and the 1960s Black Power movement. When millions of African Americans migrated from the rural South to industrial centers during and after World War II, they anticipated new opportunities for a better life. Even though they fared better in cities by earning higher wages, economic and social challenges prevailed. Discriminatory practices restricted their employment to unskilled, dirty, and low-paying menial jobs. Segregated policies in housing and the use of public facilities confined their mobility to designated areas within cities.[6] Beginning in the mid-1940s, black Americans openly protested these and other forms of racial inequalities by organizing grassroots demonstrations and boycotts. Such activities in conjunction with lawsuits filed by the NAACP contributed to the rise to the modern Civil Rights and the Black Power movements and led to modest improvements over the following two decades.[7]

The passage of the 1960s Great Society legislation and the establishment of Affirmative Action programs in the 1970s raised the expectations among African Americans for racial equality and economic and political empowerment. The emergence of funk as the most popular form of urban black musical expression in the 1970s paralleled a paradoxical era of social unrest and ubiquitous optimism that prevailed among black Americans. As a musical style, funk communicated a revolutionary spirit, an urban attitude of defiance, and black solidarity associated with the late 1960s and early1970s. Its pioneers and popularizers were from San Francisco, Los Angeles, Chicago, New York City, Brooklyn, Jersey City, Detroit, Minneapolis, Cleveland, Cincinnati, Dayton, Louisville, Atlanta, New Orleans, and Memphis. Funk is urban at its core, blending industrial-based and technological sounds with song lyrics about black urban life, the universe, and the tenets of Black Power. As such, funk is a contemporary "expression of social change, cultural liberation, and musical experimentation that revealed the resilience and creativity of African Americans under changing social [and economic] conditions."[8]

Although funk scenes existed in urban centers throughout the United States, I focus on Dayton as a case study to explore issues of identity for various reasons: (1) Dayton, a small industrial Midwestern city without the presence of a record label, became a major center for the production of funk music; (2) fourteen of the city's funk bands secured recording contracts with major labels;[9] (3) between 1968 and 1999, thirteen of these groups collectively produced 143 songs that landed on *Billboard's* R & B/Soul music charts—the most songs charted by funk groups of any one city;[10] and (4) each of these bands, as well as those without recording contracts but with local followings, evolved their own signature sound and unique persona. Despite these developments and with few exceptions,[11] Dayton Street Funk has not been the topic of comprehensive study by scholars, which has contributed to its omission from many major annals on American popular music.

Notes

1. This chapter draws and revises some material from another by the author, "Funk Music: An Expression of Black Life in Dayton, Ohio, and the American Metropolis," in *The American Metropolis: Image and Inspiration*, edited by Hans Krabbendam, Marja Roholl, and Tity de Vrie, 198–213. Amsterdam: Vu University Press, 2001, 198–213. The initial field research for this essay was conducted in 1997 and was later combined with library and archival research while a Fellow at the Center for Advanced Study in the Behavioral Sciences, (1999–2000) Stanford, California and on sabbatical (2004–2005). This essay is based primarily on extensive interviews with musicians and members of the Dayton community and in-depth analyses of sound recordings, photographs, and album jackets. I am grateful for the financial support of The Andrew W. Mellon Foundation and the College of Arts and Sciences, Indiana University-Bloomington.
2. The museum's curator, Michael Sampson, and I served as cocurators for this exhibition. Michael was responsible for collecting and labeling objects for display. My charge was to conduct research for developing a historical and socio-cultural history of Dayton Street Funk and to identify characteristic musical features as well as the innovations of the artists.
3. For a discussion and critique of this approach see: Rowena Stewart. "Bringing Private Black Histories to the Public." in *Museums and Universities: New Paths for Continuing Education*, edited by Janet W. Solinger. New York: MacMillian for National University Continuing Education Association, 1990 and Edmund B. Gaither, "'Hey! That's Mine': Thoughts on Pluralism and American Museums." in *The Politics of Public Culture: Museums and Communities*, edited by Ivan Karp, Christine Mullen Kreamer, and Steven D. Lavine, 56–64. Washington, DC: Smithsonian Institution Press, 1992.
4. Ruth Stone and Verlon Stone. "Event, Feedback, and Analysis: Research Media in the Study of Music Events." *Ethnomusicology* 25, no. 2 (1981): 215–25.
5. The Ethnomusicology Video for Instruction and Analysis Digital Archive project is an effort to establish a digital archive of ethnomusicological video for use by scholars and instructors. In addition to digitally preserving valuable ethnographic field videos of musical events, EVIA allows the original researcher to annotate their own footage, providing users with detailed explanations of the participants' activities and extensive contextual data. For more information about the project, see the EVIA website at: http://www.indiana.edu/□eviada/.
6. For a discussion of these issues, see: Lawson, Steven F. *Running for Freedom: Civil Rights and Black Politics in America Since 1941*. 2nd ed. New York: McGraw-Hill, 1977; Connolly, Harold X. *A Ghetto Grows in Brooklyn*. New York: New York University Press, 1977; Lemann, Nicholas. *The Promised Land: The Great Black Migration and How It Changed America*. New York: Alfred A. Knopf, 1991, 61–107; Sugrue, Thomas J. *The Origins of the Urban Crisis: Race and Inequality in Postwar Detroit*. Princeton: Princeton University Press, 1996. 92–123; Trotter, Jr., Joe William and Eric Ledell Smith, eds. *African Americans in Pennsylvania: Shifting Historical Perspectives*. University Park: The Pennsylvania State University Press, 1998; Katz Michael B., ed. *The "Underclass Debate": Views from History*. Princeton: Princeton University Press, 1993; Kelley, Robin D. G. "The Black Poor and the Politics of Opposition in a New South City." in *The "Underclass" Debate: Views from History*, edited by Michael B. Katz, 293–333. Princeton: Princeton University Press, 1992.
7. For accounts of these activities, see: Countryman, Matthew J. *Up South: Civil Rights and Black Power in Philadelphia*. Philadelphia: University of Pennsylvania Press, 2006; Manning, Marable. *Race, Reform, and Rebellion: The Second Black*

Reconstruction in America, 1945-1990. rev. 2nd ed. Jackson: University Press of Mississippi, 1991. 40–85; Brisbane, Robert. *Black Activism; Racial Revolution in the United States, 1954–1970.* Valley Forge, PA: Judson, 1974; Roche, John P. *The Quest for the Dream: The Development of Civil Rights in Human Relations in Modern America.* New York: Macmillan, 1963; Trotter, Jr., Joe William. *River Jordan: African American Urban Life in the Ohio Valley.* Lexington: The University of Kentucky Press, 1998. 149–50.

8.   Maultsby, Portia K. "Funk," in *The Garland Encyclopedia of World Music. Vol 3, The United States and Canada,* edited by Ellen Koskoff, 680. New York: Garland, 2001.

9.   These groups are: The Ohio Players (Westbound/Mercury), Roger (Warner/Reprise), Zapp (Warner/Reprise), Lakeside (Solor), Steve Arrington/Steve Arrington and The Hall of Fame (Atlantic), Slave (Cotillion/Atlantic), Heatwave (Epic), Sun (Liberty/Capital), Dayton (Capitol), Shadow (Elektra), Faze-O (S.H.E./Atlantic), New Horizons (Columbia), Junie (Westbound/Columbia/Island), and Platypus (Casablanca).

10.   For the charting of these groups, see Whitburn, Joel. *Joel Whitburn's Top R & B Billboard Singles 1942–2004.* Menomonee Falls, WI: Record Research, 2004.

11.   The first study of funk that devotes attention to the Dayton groups is Vincent, Rickey. *Funk: The Music, the People, and the Rhythm of the One.* New York: St. Martin's Griffin, 1996. Eight years later Scot Brown published an essay devoted to Dayton Funk, "A Land of Funk: Dayton, Ohio" in *The Funk Era and Beyond,* edited by Tony Bolden, 73–88. New York: Palgrave Macmillan, 2008.

6

The Suppression of the African Slave Trade: A Reflexive Analysis of Structural Functionalism and Cultural Relevance

James L. Conyers, Jr.

Introduction

In 1895, W.E.B. Du Bois completed his doctoral dissertation, which examined the concept of race, culture, economics, politics, and the continuity of disparate treatment of Africana phenomena. Nonetheless, the thesis of this study distinguished inequity and cultural hegemony of the African world community. Titled "The Suppression of the African Slave Trade," Du Bois's research was selected as the first publication in the Harvard Historical Studies series. C.P. Lucas describes the publication of this volume in the following: "This book is a volume of the series of Harvard historical studies. Its author, sometime fellow of Harvard University and now professor in Wilberforce University, modestly styles it in his preface, 'a small contribution to the scientific study of slavery and the American negro."[1] Additionally, John Hope Franklin offers insight by citing, "This book was, moreover, the first really distinguished scientific monograph to be published by an American Negro."[2]

In an historical perspective, Du Bois organizes this study examining colonialism's impact on Africana culture in three areas: (1) planting; (2) farming; and (3) trading. Ergo, Du Bois outlines and describes this analysis in the following: "The characteristics of the three classes of American colonies, the planting, the farming and the trading, are traced and the laws passed by each regulating or limiting that trade are summarized."[3] Located within the context of structural functionalism and cultural relevance, the effect appraisal was systemic subordination resulting from the residual effects of colonialism and involuntary migration. Truly, the consequences of these occurrences could be referred to as a teleological analysis.[4]

On the other hand, the query assessment is what variables exhibit a pattern of hindering the forward change of location of Africana phenomena. Two points of review are recorded to examine this appraisal: (1) structural functionalism and (2) cultural relevance. Equally important, structural functionalism can be defined as, "a framework for building theory that sees society as a complex system whose parts work together to promote solidarity and stability."[5] Richard Schaefer defines the functionalist perspective as "emphasiz[ing] how the parts of society are structured to maintain its stability."[6] Additionally, cultural relevance, a term coined by Alain Locke, refers to "the involvement of specific epistemological and methodological claims."[7] With the challenges of locating context and substance identified, there are fixated problems that address the advancement of African Americans. Du Bois administers discussion expressly by writing, "Thus, a social problem is ever a relation between conditions and action, and as conditions and actions vary and change from group to group from time to time and from place to place, so social problems change, develop, and grow."[8] Nevertheless, in a general context to define the term of culturalism, Peter Brooker remark upon "an examination of its lived cultural processes and the cultural texts the people of that community themselves produce and consume."[9]

Furthermore, as a sidebar with reference to studies on race and class, the terms racism, racialism, discrimination, and prejudice are often used interchangeably with a referential posited as a pattern of exclusion concerning human rights. However, all of these terms have differential that address the separation and seclusion of specified groups. Equally important, Cecil Blake describes the residual aspects of forced migration and enslavement by writing, "During enslavement and after emancipation in the United States of America, leading African spokes people agitated for emancipation and repatriation to their ancestral homeland. Their rhetorical stances and lines of argument crafted an ideology for African national development after their eventual repatriation."[10]

In summarizing the organization and structure of this critical essay, my focus is to examine three sub areas and provide a conclusion that discusses a reflection of the topic and analysis of the research and findings of Du Bois. The focus of this research essay is to provide a reflexive analysis of Du Bois's study while inspecting (1) structural functionalism and (2) cultural relevance.

Structural Functionalism

Du Bois's "The Suppression of the African Slave Trade" (New York: Library of America, 1986) was originally his doctoral dissertation at Harvard University where he was awarded a PhD degree in 1895. The first publication of this document was in 1896. Even more important, I reviewed a collection of essays written by Du Bois and compiled by Nathan Huggins. In a historical perspective, in 1896 the presidential administration of William McKinley endorsed the concept of Republicanism. Pungently, it was McKinley, who in 1900 after being reelected, supported the candidacy of Theodore Roosevelt for the presidency of the United States. The era of Republicanism enhanced a posture of conservatism in the American public sphere.

Bantering this point further, from the period of Reconstruction to the early 1930s African Americans supported the Republican Party in aggregative numbers. Ergo, the publication of Du Bois's survey handled the climate of race relations at the crossroads of separate but equal (i.e., segregation). Elliott Rudwick describes Du Bois as an African American leader citing the term propagandist—used here in its neutral meaning as denoting one who employs symbols to influence the feelings and behavior of an audience—as a particularly apt description of the role played by Du Bois, the leading black intellectual and the most important black protest spokesman in the first half of the twentieth century.[11] Steiner continues this analysis, remarking:

> We question whether Mr. DuBois is not too severe in his condemnation of the founders of our national constitution for their compromise on the slave trade. While the South had not begun to defend slavery at that time, the North also had not been inspired with that fierce indignation against the "peculiar institution" which nerved her arm to such vigorous attacks against it in later years.[12]

Du Bois by far can be considered one of the world's greatest or most prolific writers of the nineteenth and twentieth centuries. Critically, Maulana Karenga submits, "W.E.B. Dubois was an impressive leader in his own right whose rise to national and international fame was based not on white patronage, but on his own intellectual genius and role as an activist scholar."[13] Accessorial, Herbert Aptheker notes the achievements of Du Bois composing, "Dr. W.E.B. Dubois was more a history maker than an historian. The two were intertwined, however, what interested Dubois as a maker of history helped determine what he wrote and what he wrote helped make history."[14] Comparatively, Manning Marable in "W.E.B. Dubois, Radical Black Democrat" suggests in his bibliographical essay that there are three areas to locate the writings of Du Bois: (1) political journalism and social criticism; (2) scholarly and academic writings; and (3) literature and novels.

Na'im Akbar gives an informative and critical analysis of education versus training by citing, "We are saying that education is a process by which you are more actively capable of manifesting what you are. When you are increasingly manifest what somebody else wants you to be which may or may not be critical to your survival as a life form you are actually trained."[15] Lastly, Asante acknowledges Du Bois prepared the world for Afrocentricity; he wrote several articles, essays, and books to advance the position of Africana people.[16] Indeed, few scholars of this era and even those scholars in contemporary times have produced the body of scholarship amassed by Du Bois. With emphasis on the Northern colonies, he addresses their economic, political, and social mechanics to deprive of human qualities and take advantage of African people.

Admittedly, from my readings in this study I recognize Du Bois as a scholar and activist. I submit this exists for three general reasons. First, his life experiences and growing up in Great Barrington, Massachusetts— in fact, this environment allowed Du Bois to adjust to racially diverse communities. Interestingly, Marable attributes the success of Du Bois as a scholar and race man, writing: "He was an intellectual driven by his Calvinist upbringing and deep democratic ideals, who frequently opposed the dominant current of his times."[17] As a result of aggressive or unfavorable experiences in Tennessee and having the segregated community of Fisk University, Du Bois was afforded a period of reflection, empathy, and cultural understanding of the black experience. Second, Du Bois was conditioned in some way to integrated communities and understood the merits and accountability of double consciousness. Third, in distinguishing the modulations of Du Bois, he is the testimonial of the lived experience of place, space, and time. Du Bois, comparable to other African American scholars during this era, was challenged with the adversities of examining data from an alternative analysis. Last, Du Bois illustrates his flexibility as a scholar by writing and using vernacular expressiveness.

Cultural Relevance

In discussing a controversial issue such as the enslavement of Africans there is a necessity for African scholars to have the duality of effectively communicating with individuals outside and inside the academic community. Equally important, it is relevant to take a minute to provide some working explanations and analysis of the term culture and its relevance. Culture can be defined in a survey manner to discuss four aspects of human phenomena: history, ethos, mythology, and motif. Christel Temple renders, "For people of African descent, and for humanity in general, the concept of post Western is powerful because it implies that we are emerging into a period where the West ceases to be relevant as a dictator of the possibilities of our future."[18] Furthermore, William L. Van DeBurg writes about Afro-American culture and Folk Expression in the following manner:

> Black folk expression (here defined to include the visual, linguistic, and culinary arts; folklore, music, and religion) mirrored the impact which living black in a white-dominated land could have on a people. Their unique cultural expression was by no means racially exclusive in the sense that it was transmitted through genes. . . . Black culture was not deficient or deviant or a pathological perversion of mainstream culture.[19]

Bernard Steiner proceeds from this dialogue, posting:

> The various developments of the slave trade in the "planning," "farming," and "trading" colonies is well described. Attention is called to the influence which the Haitian revolt, under Toussaint l'Ouverture, had upon rigidity passage of our federal prohibitory act. We wished no slave insurrection. The international attitude of the United States receives full discussion including such topics as the proclamation of the slave trade as piracy, the question of the right of search, the quintuple treaty, and the joint squadron on the coast of Africa.[20]

In this way, to even use rhetoric, such as a monograph, which he does in the introduction of this document, illustrates the rigidness of the sources because to study or write an account of Africans being enslaved is not just an historical act, but an issue that extends itself to investigate the subject areas of religion, psychology, social organizations, politics, creative production, economics, and history. Steiner cites:

> The author has done well in disentangling the mingled political, moral, and economic elements, which run through every phase of the slavery question. He has shown that the slave trade of the Americans with Africa, was by no means confined to American ports, nor to those secluded inlets where the slavers smuggled in their captives.[21]

Observably, the enslavement of Africans is a topic that has to be examined from a systems analysis, which draws query such as, what is the axiological base of Africana historiography investigated from an alternative analysis or the merits of internationalization of examining the residual aspects of enslavement in contemporary times. Unruffled, Franklin extends appraise critically composing:

> But Dr. DuBois carries the story beyond the formal end of the African slave trade in1808. His findings reveal that there was no real settlement of the problem until after the Civil War. The act of 1807 came very near being a dead letter, he argues; and he produces abundant evidence to support his contention that the trade persisted for many decades following its formal prohibition.[22]

What is more, Du Bois trusted in the use of tools from socialist societies as instruments of evaluation to advance the position of African Americans. Even so, the use of these tools in socialist societies is not challenged by issues of physical difference in race or cultural subordination. Possibly because of his ideal scope of an objective analysis, Du Bois petitions for social science amendments regarding the restoration of the American public sphere. Franklin bestows, "This reviewer, for one, would regard the failure of Dr. DuBois to place this study of the African advert to trade in the framework of a concept of Marx on the class struggle for income and power as a most fortunate dereliction."[23]

In reviewing primary sources, Du Bois provides an alternative interpretation of Africana phenomena from an Afrocentric perspective. Nevertheless, he offers a systems analysis of the creation and consequence of subordinate group status.

Du Bois is critical of the Southern colonies' involvement in the trading and selling of Africans. Nevertheless, he refers to the Middle and New England colonies as objectivist. In the preface of this book, Du Bois is polar on the Southern colonies system of enslavement, as compared to the analysis he gives for the Northern colonies. For example, he cites that Rhode Island from the year 1700 onward became the distinguished slave trader in America. Du Bois submits a historiography that examines the written scholarship and the treatment, posture, and position of describing and evaluating the enslavement of Africans.

Moving into the latter stages of this essay, Du Bois adverts to how the war in 1776 did not cease European expansionism while they were fighting for their own independence. He notes Jefferson and his constituents never envisioned the thought of slavery existing in the future, citing Great Britain as the primary heir in the endorsement of slavery.[24] Du Bois goes on to provide information concerning the colonists' recognition of the profit in the industry of endorsing slavery.[25] He cites in 1784 the English Slave trade transported twenty thousand slaves to the West Indies. Du Bois contends the African Slave trade was brutal, immoral, and an economically profitable institution for Europeans colonialism and expansion. On the issue of the Federal Convention and the first Proposition, Du Bois focused on the debate of May 14 to June 19 1787, which focused on the representation of slaves.[26] The thought from this passage infers that the colonial forces prioritized the enforcement of enslavement over the disruption of the law of enslaving Africans.

Reflexivity and Cultural Continuity

In focusing on the analytical perspectives of paradigmatic approaches, there are three areas of concentration in the paradigmatic approaches. Marable locates the scholarly and academic writings of Du Bois, a vigilant attempt in his search for truth. Although some African scholars in contemporary times would feel it is necessary to recognize Du Bois, I contend he was Afrocentric in reviewing the axiological position of this monograph, which focuses primarily on the relativity of values and concepts. He writes a brilliant study, which redefines and reaffirms the position of Africana phenomena.

Second, epistemology determines how we measure knowledge and acquisition what is real. In this essay Du Bois offered to present this information in a social science analysis. Third, ontology defines the nature and being. In this area he identifies Africana enslavement brought about by Europeans signaled colonialism and the advancement of involuntary migration and annexation.

Finally, as mentioned in the beginning of this essay, the primary goal was to work on a reflexive essay with emphasis on the social study completed by Du Bois and focus on structural functionalism and cultural relevance. In this analysis, he has produced a body of knowledge for Africana scholars to advance within the academies and communiversities for reaffirming and redefining cultural autonomy and sovereignty.

In summary, Steiner proffers a solid analysis of the Du Bois study by writing: "Mr. DuBois has done a thoroughly good piece of work. His research has been exhaustive and accurate and he has so incorporated the results of that research that the reader has a true book and not an ill-digested collection of facts."[27]

Notes

1. Lucas, C. P. "Review Essay of 'The Suppression of the African Slave Trade to the United States of America, 1638–1870' by W.E.B. DuBois." *The English Historical Review* 12, no. 47 (July 1897): 572–574.
2. Franklin, Jon Hope. "Review Essay of 'The Suppression of the African Slave Trade to the United States of America, 1638–1870' by W.E.B. DuBois." *The Journal of Negro History* 40, no. 2 (April 1955): 182–184.

3. Du Bois, W.E.B. "The Suppression of the African Slave Trade to the United States of America, 1638–1870."*The American Historical Review* 2, no. 3 (April 1897): 55–559.
4. Beeghley, Leonard. *The Structure of Social Stratification in the United States.* Boston: Allyn and Bacon, 10.
5. *Wikipedia.* "Structural Functionalism," last modified March 12, 2013, http://en.wikipedia.org/wiki/Structural_functionalism
6. Schaefer, Richard T. *Racial and Ethnic Groups.* Upper Saddle River, New Jersey: Pearson and Prentice Hall, 2008, 116.
7. *Wikipedia.* "Cultural Relativism." last modified March 26, 2013, Http://en.wikipedia.org/wiki/Cultural_relativism
8. Bracey, John, August Meier, and Elliott Rudwick, eds. *The Black Sociologists: The First Half Century.* Belmont, California: Wadsworth Publishing, 1971, 15.
9. Brooker, Peter. *A Concise Glossary of Cultural Theory.* New York: Arnold/Oxford University Press, 1999, 47.
10. Blake, Cecil "An African Nationalist Ideology: Framed in Diaspora and the Development Quagmire." *Journal of Black Studies* 35, no. 5 (May 2005): 574
11. Franklin, John Hope and August Meir, eds, *Black Leaders of the 20th Century.* Urbana, Illinois: University of Illinois Press, 1982, 63.
12. Steiner, Bernard. "Book Review Essay." 116.
13. Karenga, Maulana. *Introduction to Black Studies.* Los Angeles: Kawaida Publications, 1983, 114.
14. Aptheker, Herbert *Afro-American History: The Modern Era.* Secacus, New Jersey: Citadel Press, 1971, 47.
15. Akbar, Na'im. *From Mis-Education to Education.* Jersey City, New Jersey: New Mind Productions, 1982, 23.
16. Asante, Molefi Kete. *Afrocentricity.* Trenton, New Jersey: Africa World Press, 1988, 16.
17. Marable, Manning. *W.E.B. Du Bois: Black Radical Democrat.* Twayne Publishers, 1986, 1.
18. Temple, Christel N. "Strategies for Cultural Renewal in an American Based Version of African Globalism." *Journal of Black Studies.* 36, no. 3 (January 2006): 301.
19. Van DeBurg, William L. *New Day in Babylon: The Black Power Movement and American Culture, 1965–1975.* Chicago: University of Chicago Press, 1992, 193.
20. Steiner, Bernard C. "Review Essay of 'The Suppression of the African Trade to the United States of America, 1638–1870,' by W.E.B. DuBois." *Annals of the American Academy of Political and Social Science* 19 (May 1897):116–118.
21. Ibid.
22. Franklin, John Hope. "Book Review Essay." 183.
23. Ibid., 184.
24. Huggins, Nathan I., ed. *Du Bois: Writings:* The Suppression of the African Slave Trade; The Souls of Black Folk; Dusk of Dawn; Essays. New York: Library of America, 1987, 53–54.
25. Ibid., 55.
26. Ibid., 58.
27. Steiner, Bernard C., 116.

7

The Big Bad Wolf: Lupus, Identity, and African American Women

Kesha Morant Williams
Ronald L. Jackson II

Introduction

In childhood nursery rhymes we learned about a *pretend* big bad wolf that blew down houses, gobbled up little pigs, and tormented a young girl and her grandmother. Few people learned about the *real* big bad wolf—lupus, which destroys autoimmune systems, causes excruciating physical pain, and inhibits any predictability to daily life. Lupus is a chronic disease that means wolf in Latin. Explanations of the disease's name range from a comparison between a butterfly rash that many lupus patients have on their cheeks and a wolf's bite and the similarity in appearance between a rash and a wolf's face to ulcers that people in the sixteenth century contracted or even a hungry wolf eating a person's face (Potter 1993). In any case the *real* big bad wolf quietly devours its prey with confusing symptoms, unpredictability, and chronic pain.

Chronic illnesses are not curable; they are a life sentence that impact daily life and interfere with the work, future goals, and social relationships of those living with the disease. Most significantly, it forces those living with chronic illnesses to renegotiate their identity (Barnado et al. 2012; Gallop et al. 2012; Low and McBride-Henry 2012; Vickers 1997). Although African American women are diagnosed with lupus more than any other population of people, there is little to no research on the lived

65

experiences of African American women living with lupus. The purpose of this exploratory study is to lay the groundwork for research documenting the experiences of those most greatly affected by this disease. In this paper, we are specifically looking at the ways in which lupus affects the participants' identities. By analyzing the themes that emerged from their collective stories we learned how the disease disrupted and reshaped the identities of the women.

What Is Lupus?

Lupus is a chronic autoimmune disease that can damage any part of the body. A healthy immune system fights off foreign bodies protecting it from viruses such as the flu as well as harmful bacteria and germs. A person living with lupus has a compromised immune system. In lupus, a person's immune system is tricked into believing that healthy tissues are unhealthy tissues or foreign bodies. The body turns against itself and causes significant harm to a person's organs and overall health. Although considerable scientific research about the causes and treatments of lupus are underway, research from the perspectives of those living with the disease is dismal (Barnado, et al. 2012; Gallop et al. 2012; Mendelson 2003; Hale, et al. 2006a and 2006b).

This disease is poorly understood by society and those living with it experience extreme periods of isolation and are often dismissed as lazy hypochondriacs. This disparaging label normally arises out of the endless list of possible symptoms lupus patients endure. It is not uncommon for multiple people living with lupus to have completely different symptoms (Gallop, et al. 2012; LFA 2012; Mendelson 2003). For example, one person living with lupus might experience joint pain and swelling, while another might have abnormal urinalysis suggesting kidney disease or problems with their nervous system such as convulsions and psychosis. Other patients have abnormalities such as inflamed lining of lungs, heart, and abdomen. The endless list of potential abnormalities leads to great difficulty when diagnosing the disease. In fact, people living with lupus are often tested for Lyme disease, HIV, and thyroid disease before lupus is even considered. The disease is often called a chameleon because many symptoms mimic those of other illnesses. According to the Center for Disease Control (CDC), lupus is one of the least recognized diseases and is one of the most difficult diseases to diagnose. The difficulty in diagnosis is linked to the fact that lupus is a criteria diagnosis disease. This means a person must meet certain criteria before diagnosis occurs (Gallop, et al. 2012; LFA 2012). There must be evidence of abnormalities in several different organ systems before a person is diagnosed with lupus. Diagnosis is usually made after a careful review of the patient's medical history and current symptoms and an analysis of lab tests (Barnado, et al. 2012; Gallop et al. 2012; Hale et al. 2006a, 2006b, and 2005). In our research we seek to identify the impact the disease has on a person's identity. What follows next is a review of relevant literature, a description of our single case study methodology, and a presentation of our analysis.

Racial Disparity

In 2011, the first lupus drug since 1955 was approved by the FDA. Unfortunately the drug is least effective for those with the greatest need as African Americans "did not appear to respond to Benlysta as well as other patients" (DeNoon 2011, para. 7). Part of this initiative involves creating additional lupus drugs. Some researchers argue that lupus research in communities of color was limited because of recruitment barriers. African Americans, in particular, have been leery to participate in any medical research because of unethical practices such as the Tuskegee Syphilis Experiment (Carrington 2000). Nevertheless African American women are three times more likely to receive a lupus diagnosis than white women. In addition African American women who are diagnosed with lupus develop the disease at an earlier age and have higher rates of lupus-related deaths than their white counterparts (Barnado et. al 2012). To combat this disproportion and lack of awareness surrounding this disease President Obama appropriated one million dollars in new funding for a national lupus program led by the Office of Minority Health (Dowd cited in LRI 2012). The Lupus Research Institute (LRI) has made it a priority to eliminate racial disparities related to lupus. The LRI strives to decrease the disparity through partnerships with the Congressional Black Caucus, congressional briefings on racial disparity in lupus, the first ever National Institute of Health (NIH) lupus research plan, and a five city series about heart disease and lupus (LRI 2012).

Lupus and Identity

Lupus flares are unpredictable and develop from an enormous list of triggers. This can lead to a life of isolation as patients silently cope with the effects of the disease. The ongoing sickness can trigger a poor quality of life for the person living with the disease as well as their loved ones. The effects of the disease can limit or disrupt their family, work, and social lives because, rather than going away, it functions in waves or periods of wellness and illness. People living with lupus usually look physically healthy and they adopt outwardly normal behaviors in public. The disease leads to isolation because patients usually experience their suffering alone (Gallop, et. al 2012; Vickers 1997). In addition to isolation, lupus also causes a biography disruption leading patients to renegotiate their identity. Biography disruption is the idea that chronic illness affects daily life, individual identity, self-reliance, and personal relationships (Bury 2008). Disease introduces discontinuity in a person's life trajectory. People living with a chronic illness have to adjust or recreate their identity. According to Jackson, Glenn, and Morant Williams (2012) people pay particular attention to and think about their identity during times of crisis or if displaced. Participants receiving a diagnosis of lupus are an example of crisis and displacement.

Lupus complications might require a person to change careers, forgo having children, or renegotiate their educational goals. The disease disrupts a person's ability to function socially or to engage in activities. The unpredictability of the disease forces many patients to adjust to a slower pace in life. Other patients assert that when they are in remission they accomplish a great deal because they are unable to when flares arise (Lowe and McBride-Henry 2012). This newly renegotiated identity leaves the people living with lupus analyzing what has been lost from their old identity, what remains the same, and what is new. The person must come to terms with their diagnosis hence adopting lupus as part of their identity.

Social Support

The effects of the disease and the identity changes that occur are often managed through social support. Those living with lupus sometimes feel isolated from the normalcy of life. Research supports that social support among African American women is higher than that in other communities and is a phenomenon others desire to emulate. According to a Washington Post/Kaiser Family Foundation poll African American women's intra-group support system adds to their high self-esteem, positivity, resilience, and self-efficacy (Czekalinski 2012; Garrett Stodghill 2012; KFF 2012; Thomas 2012). African American women are loyal to community and each other. Earlier this year the military announced that they will study "the uniquely supportive culture" and the "specific social qualities" of black women (Kemp cited in Garret Stodghill 2012, para. 1) in an effort to reduce military suicides.

It is plausible that the same commitment to social support found in face-to-face interpersonal relationships amongst African American women is also present in online social support settings. "Online social support is defined as the cognitive, perceptual, and transactional process of initiating, participating in, and developing electronic interaction or means of electronic interactions to seek beneficial outcomes in health care status, perceived health, or psychosocial processing ability" (LaCoursiere 2001, 66). Although participants cited a variety of reasons for participating in online social support groups, men were more likely to give information while women were more likely to give emotional support (LaCoursiere 2001; Mo and Coulson 2008).

Online social support offers availability and accessibility in ways that face-to-face groups cannot. Those who were once unable to participate in support groups because of distance or time constraints are now able to do so through virtual communication (Barak, Boniel-Nissim, and Suler 2008; LaCoursiere 2001). Social support is essential in the lives of people living with lupus or other chronic diseases. "Online support for those with chronic illness is a logical outgrowth of the increasing availability of the Internet and popularity of Internet communities," (Mendelson 2003, 299). Research supports (Barak, Boniel-Nissim, and Suller 2008) that the ability to share one's own story and engage in collective interaction with others who have similar lived experiences increases self-empowerment and motivates behavioral change.

Method

The general purpose of this interpretive study is to explore the ways lupus affects the identity of the participants. Through a single case study this research examines the experiences of African American women living with lupus within a private online social support group. In sharing their experiences the women offer insight into the effects of this disease and inform health researchers about an important area of culture-centered research.

The present study uses a qualitative single case study design. According to Sandelowski (2011), case studies are appropriate for person-centered care and participant-centered research. This approach allows for analysis of events and conditions and their connections to real-life occurrences. The case study approach identifies and focuses on one or more cases rather than a large number of participants.

> This allow(s) the researches to focus in-depth on the stories and themes that came out of the data. This in-depth focus, in turn, allowed the uncovering of the participant's reality, what it is really like for them on a day-to-day basis, to better understand the factions that influence, and give meaning to their lives. (Lowe and McBride-Henry 2012, 19–20)

A key strength of the case study method is the use of multiple sources of evidence and procedures when gathering data (Anderson 2011; Yin 2009). Because there is little research related to this issue, a qualitative research design provided an effective means of gleaning information.

This case study explores the experiences of eight African American women at various stages of life (ages twenty-five to fifty) living with lupus. The purposive sample was identified through social media announcements, interpersonal relationships, and a lupus association email list serv. The participants were included because they are African American women who have been diagnosed with lupus. Participants provided informed consent in compliance with the Institutional Review Board requirements and did not receive direct payment for participation.

Group Characteristics: Portraits of Participants

Pseudonyms are used for all study participants. The women in the research include: (1) *Charlene*, thirty-three years old, single parent, and nursing student; (2) *Emilee*, twenty-nine years old, married, mother of two young children; (3) *London*, thirty-two years old, married, mother of one, and step mother of two; (4) *Shayna*, forty years old, divorced, mother of a preteen and a new teen, and clinical counselor; (5) *Janiece*, twenty-five years old, youth coordinator, and nursing student; (6) *Brianna*, thirty-two years old, doctoral student, senior admissions counselor, and guardian of her brother and young niece; (7) *Tara*, fifty years old, married, mother of three adult children, and grandmother of one; (8) *Erin*, thirty-six years old, divorced and remarried, mother of two adopted children and one step child.

Table 1

Pseudo Name	Diagnosis/ Year	Age	Relation- ship Status	Children/ Guardian- ship	Education Level	Career
Charlene	SLE, Pulmonary Fibrosis, Protein S. deficiency/ Diagnosed 2009	33	Single	Son 7	Enrolled in BSN program	Student
Emilee	SLE, Rheumatoid Arthritis/ Diagnosed 2010	29	Married	Daughters 1½, 6	MA	Speech Pathologist
London	SLE, Discoid Lupus, Dermato- myositis/ Diagnosed 2004–05	32	Married	Daughter 6, Step daughter/ son 11, 9	BA	Professional Recruiter
Shayna	SLE, Sjogren's Syndrome, Raynaud's Disease/ Diagnosed 2005	40	Divorced	Daughter 12, Son 14	MA (enrolled in PhD program)	Therapist/ Counselor
Janiece	SLE/ Diagnosed 2007	25	Single	No Children	Enrolled in BSN program	Youth Program Coordinator
Brianna	Discoid Lupus, Diagnosed 2010	32	Single	Brother 19, Niece 10 (Guardian- ship)	MA (enrolled in PhD program)	University Admissions Officer
Tara	SLE, Sjogren's Syndrome/ Diagnosed 2006	50	Married	Sons 27, 24, Daughter 23	BA	Human Resources/ Accounting
Erin	SLE/ Diagnosed 2012	36	Divorced/ Remarried	Son 16, Daughter 10, Stepson 22 (all from first marriage)	Certifi- cation	Hospital Lab Technician

Following the principles of grounded theory, this research will allow the voices of the participants and themes to emerge from the text. Their stories, collected through participant observation of discussion, written responses to relevant question prompts, open-ended surveys, and partici-pant responses to lupus messages in an online support group, establish the voice of this research (Berkenkotter, Huckin, and Ackerman 1988; Gold and Clapp 2011; Lauer and Asher 1988). The data was collected over a three-month period. Participants received a private invitation to join the online social support group. The women were aware that the group was created to conduct a case study for a research project about lupus. This closed group was only accessible to those participating in the study. The women received a welcome message that explained the purpose and guide-lines of the research. To begin they were asked to introduce themselves and share their diagnosis stories. In addition, valuable information came from impromptu conversations between the women offering support and suggestions to each other.

Grounded theory and a qualitative content analysis are used to allow the dominant themes to emerge from the text. Grounded theory was used because the interpretive process allows the themes to emerge inductively from the text. The interpretative process of analyzing the text was per-formed in three phases: preparation, organizing, and reporting (Elo and Kynga 2007). In the preparation phase, the transcripts from the online support group were read multiple times to achieve an overall sense of the content. Next, the text was read for content that specifically related to participant identity.

The organizing phase included open coding, creating categories, and abstraction. After repeated readings of the text, recurrent manifest and latent concepts were coded. The codes and in-process memos were writ-ten directly in the margins of the transcripts of online support group (Elo and Kynga 2007; Hsieh and Shannon 2005; Lindlorf and Taylor 2002). A coding sheet with the codes and in-process memos was created. After completing the open coding, categories were generated through the abstraction process. The categories were grouped and then collapsed based on similarities and differences.

Finally, in the reporting stage the researchers analyzed the process and the results of the study. Examining the validity and reliability of the case study is essential (Yin 2009). Validity was established by using multiple sources of evidence (e.g., participant observation of discussion, written responses to relevant question prompts, open-ended surveys, personal drawings, and participant responses to lupus messages in an online support group) and through member checks with research participants. For the member check the case study information was summarized in an e-mail and sent to participants. The participants were asked to reply to the e-mail supporting or discrediting the accuracy of the summary (Lindlorf and Taylor 2002). The development of a case study protocol and a case study database add to the reliability of this study. To establish credibility and transferability we followed Ratcliff's (1995) model by making comparisons with relevant literature and extensive quotation from the text.

Who Am I? Lupus and Identity

In this analysis we explore emergent themes that address participant interpretations of the ways in which lupus affect their identity. The emergent themes that directly related to identity included disruption, evolution, embrace, and support system.

Themes

Disruption. A disruption interrupts the normal course or unity—to be thrown into disorder. The signs and symptoms of lupus are a disruption to the participant's identity because it forces them to change or modify actions they once considered a significant part of who they were. For example, London shared that prior to being affected by lupus she was heavily involved in athletic activities; however, at twenty-seven years old her physical ability to engage in athletics vanished.

> My athletic body lost ALL its muscle (50lbs lost) sagging skin and (TMI) a concave butt. I was an 80-year-old in a 27-year-old body. (London)

In another example Brianna shares that lupus has halted her ability to enjoy the sun. In her pre-lupus life she loved the beach, cookouts, and other outdoor events. Since her diagnosis she is cautious about her sun exposure hence limiting her ability to do something she enjoys.

> The disease requires that I stay out the sun. This is another major change for me because I am one brown woman that enjoys tanning and fun in the sun. I now have to enjoy the sun in shorter intervals and must use sunscreen. (Brianna)

London and Brianna's experiences echoed the experiences of the other women in this case study. Their responses also support life disruption and chronic illness literature that posits people living with chronic illness have to adjust or recreate their identity.

Evolution. Evolution is defined as a process of continuous change in a certain direction. The stories of our participants highlight the continuous change they experienced prior to and during their diagnosis. In all cases the women described a process. When thinking back on early signs and symptoms, some felt physically fatigued and achy, others had legions, and a few experienced brain fog. In the majority of cases the women suffered with increased and more substantial health changes for years before diagnosis. When reflecting back, Shayna now recognizes lupus symptoms she experienced over twenty years ago.

> I can trace a lot of symptoms back to 1990 when I was in college and in 1998 when I was in the Army. Headaches, pleurisy. (I was rushed to the hospital, felt like a heart attack). When my son was about 5 [and] learning how to ride a bike, I was running behind him holding the bike. Later that day and several days afterwards, I was so sore and felt like I had pulled several muscles. I couldn't understand why it felt like every muscle in every part my body. I couldn't walk or do much of anything and felt like I was out of shape. Fast forward several years, I now realize that I had sent my body into a spinning Lupus flare! (Shayna)

In other cases the participants do not recall early signs and symptoms, however, their introduction to lupus was abrupt, life altering, and almost deadly. Janiece was an undergraduate student and an area hospital employee when one day she got sick. Although her diagnosis was quick and did not come after years of testing, the massive changes she has experienced since diagnosis have evolved her into a new person.

> The day of my diagnosis was August 1, 2007. My kidneys completely failed due to SYE Lupus. My kidneys were only working 10% all together. When I first went into the emergency room on August 1, 2007 my creatinine was 11.2. (At 12 you're dead.) I was on dialysis for 20 months. I did peritoneal dialysis, which was a port located in my perineum. My dialysis would go through the port in my stomach and I had to do it 7 days a week for 9 hours a day. My sister gave me her kidney and that was on one the biggest things that she could have done to support me. I have had my kidney for 3 years now and my creatinine is at a 9! I'm blessed and grateful. (Janiece)

Brianna introduces fear and the question of "what if" into the process of evolution. Her comment directly addresses a thought that many of the women indirectly hint at in their responses. What if this doesn't get better? What if it gets worse? What if I die? At present, Brianna is diagnosed with discoid lupus. Discoid lupus only affects skin, causing legions and pain. However, people who are diagnosed with discoid lupus are highly likely to develop SLE, which affects your autoimmune system.

> The one very scary thing is that this Lupus can develop/worsen into another form. One of my dear friends lost her mother to the disease. She remembers her mother's Lupus

> beginning with discoid Lupus. Although there is no guarantee that will happen, that has been the part that keeps me stressed the most. (Brianna).

It is likely that other African American women living with lupus share similar evolution stories. Literature supports that African American women develop lupus at younger ages and are more likely to die from the disease than any other population of people. Just as concerning, African American women respond poorly to the only lupus drug that has been released since 1955.

Embrace

After the women come to terms with the disruption and evolution that lupus causes in their lives, many seemed to embrace the disease as part of their journey. All of the women expressed comfort in finally receiving a diagnosis. With a diagnosis the women are better able to plan their lives and come to terms with the new component of their identity. Not only has Shayna mentally embraced her journey with lupus, but she also uses it as an opportunity to advocate for more research and to increase awareness.

> I wear pins, t-shirts and explain to others when they ask questions related to lupus. I chose to get a tattoo that represents the butterfly and a lupus ribbon with an inscription "Be Still" because although lupus creates challenges, it has also created a sense of appreciation for life. I can enjoy each day for what it is and actively seek peace and calmness because otherwise I run the risk of experiencing a flare. (Shayna)

Brianna described that large legions on her ears and neck as what led her to the dermatologist and to a diagnosis of discoid lupus. The legions drew unwanted stares or uninvited questions. She eventually adjusted to the stares and uses her pleasant personality to turn the uncomfortable moments into teaching moments.

> Thanking God that my personality has gotten me quickly pass the appearance of the legions. I am now able to speak freely about the disease when people ask what the legions are or if I catch someone looking at them but not willing to ask. (Brianna)

Similarly, London describes overcoming the reactions others had to the visible effects the disease had on her hair and skin. In her comments London uses language such as "my blushy cheeks" (i.e., butterfly rash) that embraces her difference and accepts the visible manifestation of lupus as part of her new self.

Yes I have very thin spotty hair. ([I've] been wearing a wig or weave for the past 6 years.) And my skin is fifty-eleven colors. I am use to looking crazy when I don't have 10lbs of make-up on. LOL! [laugh out loud]. The most important thing is that I have my life and my strength back. (London)

While all of the women welcome a cure for lupus, they have found peace in their current journeys. Literature supports that African American women are resilient and appear to overcome tremendous adversity yet continue to thrive. The same resilience is found in the story of each participant. Although none of the women enjoy the health repercussions or pain that come with the disease, they have adjusted to lupus and its impact upon their lives.

Support Systems

The most striking aspect of this research was the selfless social support the women in this case study offered each other. Although each woman struggled with the havoc lupus caused in their individual life, their ability to offer informational and emotional support to others who they only know through a computer screen was noteworthy. The wide range of lived experiences created an environment where newly diagnosed women could ask questions and express concerns about living with lupus. When Erin who was diagnosed with SLE one week before joining the group she learned that she would have to postpone her attempt to have a baby, and the group offered words of encouragement and advice.

So I went to the Rheumatologist on Monday and she told me that I should put my baby plans on hold because of the medicine she wants me to start.: (Broke my heart because I have been trying for over a year. Anyway, today is my second day on steroids and I keep peeing (TMI). My legs and feet feel like they are swollen and ache sooo badly. They feel like they're throbbing. I start my new medicine next week. (Erin)

Erin's post prompted ten responses of support and information about medicine and decision making from the other participants. For example, London, who had also been told to postpone attempts to conceive another child, empathized with Erin.

I know it is heartbreaking because a woman's body give us that urge to want children no matter if it is a good idea or not. What medicine are they talking about? I was on Imuran and Plaquenil and was told to get off of both if I ever considered more [children]. Hopefully, the medicine will do what it needs to do and you can get switched over to something milder. (London)

In a later response Erin asked the group members about their familiarity with the medicines she was prescribed. Her words suggested that she was confused and overwhelmed by her recent diagnosis and was encouraged by the support of her more experienced "lupy sisters." In response group members offered links to websites and open discussion groups that would give her a clearer understanding of lupus.

The availability and access of the online virtual support group provided access and community to some participants in ways that face-to-face groups could not. For example, the asynchronous discussion took place throughout their entire day. The messages were posted from computers, notepads, and cellular phones. The virtual group also provides an opportunity for collective interaction not found in all communities. The closest thriving lupus support groups to the cities Shayna, Tara, Janiece, and Charlene live in are nearly an hour away from their homes. Shortly after her diagnosis Shayna connected with a hospital in her community to start a lupus support group; however, after months of trying to rally interest she decided to find support through other outlets. Finally, the ability to reread discussion posts enhances the participant's ability to share her own story, which builds upon a larger collective story of African American women living with lupus.

Discussion and Conclusion

The present study explores an area of health communication that has been virtually ignored in the literature. Specifically, we examined what effect lupus has on participant identity. Using a single case study we examined identity and lupus through participant observation of group discussions, written responses to relevant question prompts, open-ended surveys, personal drawings, and participant responses to lupus messages in an online support group.

Lupus is a chronic autoimmune disease that affects African American women three times more often than their white counterparts. African American women are diagnosed at younger ages and are more likely to die due to lupus-related complications than any other population of people. This is particularly troubling because lupus is a disease that is poorly understood, its research is underfunded, and its most recent treatment option does not respond well to those most greatly affected by the disease—African American women. Previous research (Brower 2005) suggests that, until recently, lupus has remained under the radar because it does not have a strong advocacy campaign or a public celebrity face to attach to the cause. This lack of exposure and understanding of the disease motivates patients to find other ways to cope with the significant changes to their identity.

In the present study, the analysis revealed four themes directly related to participant identity. These themes included disruption, evolution, embrace, and support system. Manifestations of disruption explored the major shifts lupus demanded of the participants. Their normal course of life, the activities they loved to participate in, or the food they loved to eat were not off limits. Their lives were thrown into disorder. Although the disease goes through periods of remission, the remnants are always lingering. The participant must live the rest of her life being conscious of the foods, products, or activities they must resist in attempt to avoid a flare.

As a person living with a chronic disease, the participants are engrossed in a never-ending process of change. The evolution of the disease within the participants' life is directly connected to her identity. Once diagnosed, many participants finally made connections between the odd symptoms they had experienced for years and the disease. Some participants struggled with the evolution of the disease because it limits their ability to engage with their children and other loved ones.

With time many of the participants actually embraced lupus as a part of their identity in a mostly positive manner. The women expressed that there was comfort in knowing what exactly was wrong with them. Although lupus manifests differently in each person, they were thankful to have clarity about the cause of their ailments. With diagnosis they were better able to understand their limitations and adjust to the shifts in their daily lives.

Although traditional face-to-face lupus support groups are available in major cities, a number of case study participants expressed feelings of isolation in their local communities and the fact that the closest face-to-face groups are approximately an hour drive from their home. Online social support groups are a viable alternative for patients seeking social support when there is a lack of availability in their local communities but also when there are time constraints, other commitments, or a need for support outside of traditional group hours.

Limitations and Implications

A potential limitation of this study is the use of one single case study. Future research should explore this topic using multiple case studies and/or triangulated approaches. Future studies may also benefit from comparing populations. While the medical effects of lupus are heavily researched in other disciplines, our exhaustive search produced few articles that directly addressed patient perspectives of lupus in a community of social support (see Mendelson 2003). Therefore, this research creates groundwork in this virtually ignored area of health communication and culture. Additionally, this study draws attention to the ways that lupus shifts the identity of those most greatly affected by the disease. This study extends the literature on the value of social support among African American females. Living with lupus is a life sentence of confusing symptoms, unpredictability, and chronic pain. Understanding how this affects a person's identity could influence medication compliance and improve the patient's quality of life.

References

Anderson, R. "Making a Case for the Case Study Method." *Journal of Nursing Education* 59, no. 8 (2011): 427–8, doi:10.3928/01484834-20110719-01.

Barak, A., M. Boniel-Nissim, and J. Suler. "Fostering Empowerment in Online Support Groups." *Computers in Human Behavior* 24 (2008): 1867–1883, doi:10.1016/j.chb.2008.02.004.

Barnado, A., L. Wheless, A. K. Meyer, G. S. Gilkeson, and D. L. Kamen. "Quality of Life in Patients with Systemic Lupus Erythematosus (SLE) Compared with Related Controls within Unique African American Population. *Lupus* 21 (2012): 563–569, doi:10.1177/0961203311426154.

Berkenkotter, C., T. Huckin, and J. Ackerman. "Social Context and Socially Constructed Texts: The Initiation of a Graduate Student into a Writing Research Community, in *Textual Dynamics and the Professions*, edited by C. Bazerman and J. Paradis, 191–215. Madison, WI: University of Wisconsin Press, 1991.

Bury, M. "Chronic Illness as Biography Disruption." *Sociology of Health and Illness* 4, no. 2 (2008): 167–182. doi: 10.111/1467-9566.ep11339939.Center for Disease Control. www.cdc.org.

Czekalinski, S. "Black Women Key to Easing Military Suicides?" *National Journal*. (June 12, 2012) http://www.nationaljournal.com/thenextamerica/culture/black-women-key-to-easing-military-suicides--20120612

DeNoon, D. J. "New Lupus Drug Benlysta Approved." *WebMD Health News.* (March 9, 2011) http://Lupus.webmd.com.

Elo, S. and H. Kynga. "The Qualitative Content Analysis Process." *Journal of Advance Nursing* 62 no. 1 (2007): 107–115.

Gallop, K., A. Nixon, P. Swinburn, K. L. Sterling, A. N. Naegeli, and M. E. T. Silk "Development of a Conceptual Model of Health-Related Quality of Life for Systemic Lupus Erythematosus (SLE) from the Patients' Perspective." *Lupus* 21, no. 9 (2012) 934–943. dio:10.1177/ 0961203312441980.

Gold, C. L. and R. A. Clapp. "Negotiating Health and Identity: Lay Healing, Medicinal Plants, and Indigenous Healthscapes in Highland Peru." *Latin American Research Review* 46, no. 3 (2011): 93–111. doi:10.1353/lar.2011.0053.

Garrett Stodghill, A. "Black Women's Culture of Social Support to Be Studies for Prevention of Military Suicides." *The Grio.* (June 22, 2012) http://thegrio.com/2012/06/13/black-womens-culture-of-social-support-to-be-studied-for-prevention-of-military-suicides/.

Hale, E. D., G. J. Treharne, A. C. Lyons, Y. Norton, S. Mole, D. L. Mitton, K. M. J. Douglas, N. Erb, and G. D. Kitas. "Joining the Dots for Patients with Systematic Lupus Erythematosus: Personal Perspectives of Health Care from a Qualitative Study." *Ann Rheum Dis* 65 (2006a): 585–589.

————. "Concealing the Evidence: The Importance of Appearance Concerns for Patients with Systematic Lupus Erythematosus." *Lupus* 15 (2006b): 532–540. doi:10.1191/0 961203306lu2310xx.

Hsieh, H. F. and S. E. Shannon. "Three Approaches to Qualitative Content Analysis." *Qualitative Health Research* 15 (2005) 1277–1288. doi:10.1177/1049732305276687.

Jackson, R., C. Glenn, and K. M. Morant Williams. "Self Identity." In *Inter/Cultural Communication: Representation and Construction of Culture in Everyday Interaction*, edited by Anastacia Kurylo. Thousand Oaks, CA: Sage, 2012.

Kaiser Family Foundation. "Black Women in American." Last modified May 17, 2012. http://www.kff.org/kaiserpolls/8271.cfm.

LaCoursiere, S. P. "A Theory of Online Social Support." *Advances in Nursing Science* 24, no. 1 (2001): 60–77.

Lauer, J. M. and W. J. Asher. *Case Studies. Composition Research: Empirical Designs*. New York: Oxford University Press, 1998.

Lindlorf, T. R. and B. C. Taylor, B. C. *Qualitative Communication Research Methods*. Thousand Oaks, CA: Sage, 2002.

Lowe, P. and K. McBride-Henry. "What Factors Impact upon the Quality of Life of Elderly Women with Chronic Illnesses: Three Women's Perspectives." *Contemporary Nurse* 41, no. 1 (2012): 18–27. doi:10.5172/conu.2012.41.1.18.

Lupus Foundation of America (LFA). (2012). www.lupus.org.

Lupus Research Initiative (LRI). (2012) www.lupusresearchinitiative.org.

Mo, P. K. H. and N. S. Cuolson. "Exploring the Communication of Social Support within Virtual Communities: A Content Analysis of Messages Posted to an Online HIV/AID Support Group." *CyberPsychology and Behavior* 11, no. 3 2008): 371–374. doi:10.1089/cpb.2007.0118.

Mendelson, C. "Gentle Hugs: Internet List Servs as Sources of Support for Women with Lupus." *Advances in Nursing Science* 26, no. 4 (2003): 299–306.

Potter, B. *The History of a Disease Called Lupus*. New York: Oxford University Press, 1993.

Ratcliff, D. "Validity and Reliability in Qualitative Research." *Qualitative Research Resources*. (1995) http://qualitativeresearch.ratcliffs.net/Validity.pdf.

Sandelowski, M. "Casing the Research Case Study." *Research in Nursing and Health* 34 (2011): 153–159. doi: 10.1002/nur.20421.

Schudrich, W., D. Gross, and J. Rowshandel. "Psychosocial Impact of Lupus: Social Work's Role and Function." *Social Work in Health Care* 51, no. 7 (2012): 627–639. doi: 10.1080/00981389. 2012.683694.

Thompson, K. "Survey Paints Portrait of Black Women in America." *Washington Post*. (December 22, 2011) http://www.washingtonpost.com/politics/survey-paints-portrait-of-black-women-in-america/2011/12/22/gIQAvxFcJQ_story_3.html.

Vickers, M. H. "Life at Work with 'Invisible' Chronic Illness (ICI): The 'Unseen,' Unspoken, Unrecognized Dilemma of Disclosure." *Journal of Workplace Learning* 9, no. 7 (1997): 240–252.

Yin, R. K. *Case Study Research and Design and Methods*. Thousand Oaks, CA: Sage Publications, 2009.

8

Steele and the Supreme Court's Creation of the Union's Duty of Fair Representation

Ronald Turner[1]

I. Introduction

On December 18, 1944 the Supreme Court of the United States issued its seminal decision in *Steele v. Louisville & Nashville Railroad Co.*[2] Decided the same day as the Court's infamous validation of the internment of persons of Japanese descent in *Korematsu v. United States*[3] and ten years before *Brown v. Board of Education*,[4] the *Steele* Court held that a labor union acting as the exclusive collective bargaining representative for a craft or class of employees has a "duty to exercise fairly the power conferred upon it in behalf of all those for whom it acts, without hostile discrimination against them."[5]

This essay examines *Steele* and the efforts of Charles Hamilton Houston and his cocounsel, Arthur D. Shores and Joseph C. Waddy, to persuade the Court that black workers had a right to be free from and to challenge the racially discriminatory practices and conduct of their nominal union representative, the Brotherhood of Locomotive Firemen and Enginemen.

II. The Backdrop

Bester William Steele, "a Negro fireman," began working for the Louisville & Nashville Railroad in 1910 and remained in that job classification through early April 1941.[6] Steele and other black and white firemen employed by the Railroad were exclusively represented for purposes of collective bargaining by the Brotherhood—"represented" even though they were excluded from union membership by the Brotherhood's constitution and customs.[7]

In March 1940 the Railroad and twenty other railroad companies operating in the southeastern region of the United States received from the Brotherhood notice of the union's desire to amend the existing collective bargaining agreement. "By established practice on the several railroads so notified only white firemen can be promoted to serve as engineers, and the notice proposed that only 'promotable,' i.e., white, men should be employed as firemen or assigned to new runs or jobs or permanent vacancies in established runs or jobs."[8] This notice and proposed change, served on the Railroad without notice to the black firemen, would exclude all black firemen from the service.

Thereafter, in February 1941, the Brotherhood and the railroads entered into a new collective bargaining agreement, which provided that black firemen could constitute no more than 50 percent of the firemen in a class of service, with new runs and vacancies to be filled by white men until that percentage was reached, and that black workers were not to be employed in any seniority district in which they were not working. A supplemental agreement entered into in May 1941 established additional restrictions on black firemen's seniority rights and employment opportunities. Both agreements were discussed and put into effect without any notice to the black firemen and without affording them an opportunity to be heard.[9]

The injury inflicted upon and the harm suffered by Steele was immediate and harmful. He worked in the "highly preferable job" of fireman on a passenger train assigned to what was called the "South End Passenger Pool."[10] In early February 1941 all jobs in that pool were declared vacant and Steele's employer and labor representative "disqualified all the Negro firemen and replaced them with four white men, members of the Brotherhood, all junior in seniority to [Steele] and no more competent or worthy."[11] Initially displaced from his fireman job for sixteen days, Steele was reassigned to more difficult and lesser paying work on a local freight service run. He was then replaced by a white worker who had less seniority than Steele and was again reassigned, this time to a switch engine position. Thereafter, on January 3, 1942 (the date of the filing of his lawsuit against the Railroad and the Brotherhood), Steele was moved back to his original passenger service job.[12]

Steele's lawsuit sought an injunction against the enforcement of the Railroad-Brotherhood agreements and against the Brotherhood's purported representation of Steele and other similarly situated black workers "so long as the discrimination continues, and so long as it refuses to give them notice and hearing with respect to proposals affecting their interests," and requested an award of damages against the Brotherhood.[13] The defendants argued that even if the facts alleged in the suit were true and correct, Steele was not entitled to prevail; agreeing with that position, Alabama Circuit Court Judge E. M. Creel dismissed the case. Houston appealed the dismissal to the Alabama Supreme Court and appeared before that court on November 24, 1943, becoming the first black lawyer to present an oral argument to that institution.[14]

The Alabama Supreme Court affirmed the trial court's dismissal of Steele's complaint. The court opined that the federal Railway Labor Act of 1926 (RLA or Act)[15] "placed a mandatory duty upon the Railroad to treat with the representative of the employees and with that representative only."[16] Moreover, the court noted, § 152 of the RLA provided that the majority of a class or craft of employees had the right to determine the exclusive bargaining representative for that craft or class[17] and empowered that representative "to treat with the Railroad in regard to rates of pay, working conditions, and the like, and to bargain with reference to the whole without any notion of liability to the individual."[18] Accordingly, the court concluded, "the Brotherhood was the true representative, with which the Railroad was under duty to confer and negotiate,"[19] the union had the right and power to enter into the February 1941 agreement with the Railroad, and Steele "must be held to abide by the contract made with his recognized statutory representative."[20]

If the Brotherhood was in fact Steele's representative, what was the legal relationship between Steele and the union? The court made clear that it "mean[t] to indicate a representative in a limited sense only."[21]

> [T]o our mind it seems entirely clear that Congress, in providing for collective bargaining by representative of a craft or class, had no intention of creating a confidential relationship of principal and agent, such as would place a duty upon the agent to give notice to every employee of any action which might unfavorably affect him, and to make a due account for his actions, and be subject to liability for failing to so account.[22]

As noted earlier, Steele was represented by a labor organization that purposefully excluded him and other black workers from membership.[23] That a black worker was subjected to and subordinated by a representational regime in which his "true representative" openly and invidiously discriminated against African Americans is and should have been seen as a troubling, insupportable, and indefensible proposition of law. But the Alabama Supreme Court was blind or indifferent to this sociolegal reality. Acknowledging that Steele could not become a member of the Brotherhood, the state high court referenced and relied on a New Jersey appellate court decision, which stated that a union's "right to prescribe qualifications for membership and to make rules and regulations for the transaction of their lawful business is not open to question. . . . Enforced admission to membership is manifestly contrary to the scheme of such a society. No person has an abstract or absolute right to such membership."[24] In addition, the Alabama court noted that in another case the United States Court of Appeals for the District of Columbia expressed the following view: "That the rules of the Brotherhood make negroes ineligible to membership is not a matter which concerns us."[25]

In another passage of its opinion the Alabama Supreme Court stated:

> [Steele's complaint] discloses a traditional policy of the railroads throughout the country to promote to the position of engineer white firemen only. This means, of course, that such course had been considered by the management as wise and proper throughout the history of the railroads in America. [Steele] has long been in the service, and knew of this unbroken custom. He therefore knew that he would not be eligible for promotion to the position of engineer. So uniform a custom, therefore, recognized in the practical construction of his contract of employment, must be considered as a part thereof. . . .[26]

The court concluded: "If the [Railroad] considers it wise to continue the policy of having only white engineers, there is no more a law standing in the way of the exercise of this freedom of choice than there is in the choice of the Brotherhood of its membership. And it is clear enough the courts have no power to declare otherwise or to dictate a different policy."[27] Lest there be any doubt about its position on the legality of the Railroad's and Brotherhood's overt discrimination against black workers, the court devoted a paragraph of its opinion to *Plessy v. Ferguson*[28] and the Supreme Court's "many observations . . . concerning laws related to the separation of races. That it is a question of much delicacy, history teaches and all men know."[29]

III. The Interpretive Task and Argument

Seeking the United States Supreme Court's review of the Alabama Supreme Court's decision, Houston and his cocounsel filed a petition for a writ of certiorari with the nation's high court. The petition argued, among other things, that the RLA imposed a fiduciary duty on an exclusive collective bargaining representative to represent all members of the craft fairly and impartially.[30] The United States Congress created the relationship "between the collective bargaining and grievance representative and the members of the craft it represents under the Railway Labor Act," the petition stated, and "[i]f Congress established a confidential relationship between the representative and the workers, and imposed fiduciary duties on the representative to represent all members of the craft impartially, [Steele] has undoubtedly stated a cause of action."[31] Houston argued that the Brotherhood had a legal duty and obligation to represent Negro firemen and to give those workers notice, an opportunity to be heard, the chance to vote on proposed policies adversely affecting their interests, prompt and full disclosure of all union actions, and freedom from discrimination.[32]

The argument that the RLA imposed on unions a duty of fair representation presented an interesting question of statutory interpretation. As no such duty was expressly set forth in the text of the statute, the source of an employee's asserted right to freedom from discrimination by his or her union representative presented an interpretive and applicative puzzle.

Did Congress intend to grant an RLA-designated union representative the power to represent a majority of employees with no concern or regard for the minority? One approach to statutory interpretation, known as intentionalism, seeks to discern the meaning of a statutory provision as held by the enacting legislature and legislators. One analyst has suggested that in determining the relevant intent a judge attempts to "put himself in the shoes of the enacting legislators and figure out how they would have wanted the statute applied to the case before him."[33] This approach has been criticized as searching for an "obvious fiction": the intent of a multimember legislature whose members did not or may not have had any specific intent with regard to the specific issue before the court.[34] Did the Congresses that enacted the RLA in 1926 and amended that statute in 1934 intend to outlaw union discrimination against black workers? According to one commentator, "Congress knew that the unions to which it was granting tremendous power in 1926 and 1934 were exclusionary, and it obviously had no strong objection to the unions' policies."[35]

Another approach to statutory interpretation, purposivism, identifies a statute's purpose and determines which interpretation best fits or is the most consistent with that purpose or goal.[36] A purposivist interpreter derives statutory meaning "from an understanding of what social problems the legislature was addressing and what general ends it was seeking."[37] This approach assumes that a judge can determine a statute's pertinent purpose. Where that purpose is explicitly codified in the text of the statute the relevant purpose may be obvious and the jurist seeking to resolve a legal dispute is provided with sufficient, if not determinative, guidance.

But where a statute does not contain an express declaration of purpose, or has more than one stated purpose, "the assumption that the judge can authoritatively determine the law's relevant and operative purpose or purposes is a problematic proposition."[38] Was union discrimination against black workers consistent with or contrary to the RLA's purposes and policies?

Going beyond the RLA, the petition stated that the Congressional grant of power to the Brotherhood to act as the exclusive bargaining representative for the entire craft or class, and the union's exercise of that power, were subject to the Fifth Amendment of the United States Constitution.[39] Placing "the minority members' jobs at the absolute and unrestrained power of the representative . . . with no guiding standards, would be an unconstitutional delegation of legislative power and derivation of liberty and property without due process of law."[40] Not subjecting that power to constitutional restraints would "place the Negro firemen in economic serfdom to the Brotherhood . . . It is unthinkable that Congress, itself the creature of representative government with limitations both written and implied, did not use the word *representative* in the Railway Labor Act in the sense of creating such representative [as] the agent or servant of the workers it represents, with a duty to represent the entire class impartially."[41]

In the concluding paragraph of the petition Houston set forth his views on the negative and potentially violent consequences of not addressing and outlawing the discriminatory conduct challenged by Steele.

> Repeatedly the effects of the white firemen to drive the Negro firemen out of service have broken out in violence. The records are recorded in the Federal Archives; the testimony was taken before the President's Committee on Fair Employment Practice in September, 1943; before the Select Committee of the House of Representatives to Investigate Executive Agencies (Smith Committee) in March, 1944. The seeds of industrial warfare which will adversely affect the war effort are present. It is paramount in the public interest that the rights and duties of the collective bargaining and grievance representative under the Railway Labor Act be determined peaceably by the Courts, since no other forum for hearing and determination of the problem exists . . . rather than risk the interruption to commerce and attendant evils by settling the question by violence.[42]

On May 29, 1944, the Supreme Court granted Steele's petition.[43] (Interestingly, it appears that Houston never filed a brief on the merits with the Supreme Court.[44]) Oral argument was heard on November 14, 1944, with Houston making his third argument to the Court.[45] Justice William O. Douglas observed that Houston "was a veritable dynamo of energy guided by a mind that had as sharp a cutting edge as any I have known," and that Houston's argument in *Steele* was "one of his best."[46]

IV. The Supreme Court's Decision

On December 18, 1944 the Supreme Court issued its decision. Writing for the Court, Chief Justice Harlan Fiske Stone framed the issue as follows: whether the RLA "imposes on a labor organization, acting by authority of the statute as the exclusive bargaining representative of a craft or class of railway employees, the duty to represent all the employees in the craft without discrimination because of their race, and, if so, whether the courts have jurisdiction to protect the minority of the craft or class from the violation of such obligation."[47]

At the outset, the Court noted that the Alabama Supreme Court's conclusion that the RLA imposed no legal obligation or duty on the Brotherhood to protect minority workers from discrimination or unfair treatment gave rise to constitutional questions.

> For the representative is clothed with power not unlike that of a legislature which is subject to constitutional limitations on its power to deny, restrict, destroy or discriminate against the rights of those for whom it legislates and which is also under an affirmative constitutional duty equally to protect those rights. If the Railway Labor Act purports to impose on [Steele] and the other Negro members of the craft the legal duty to comply with the terms of a contract whereby the representative has discriminatorily restricted their employment for the benefit and advantages of the Brotherhood's own members, we must decide the constitutional questions which petitioner raises in his pleadings.[48]

Avoiding the constitutional questions noted in the above-quoted text,[49] the Court turned its attention instead to the RLA and, more specifically, to its understanding of Congressional intent relative to that statute. In the Court's view, Congress "did not intend to confer plenary power upon the union to sacrifice, for the benefit of its members, rights of the minority of the craft, without imposing on it any duty to protect the minority."[50] As Steele and other black members of the craft were not and could not be members of the Brotherhood,[51] the union's authority to represent them for purposes of collective bargaining was "derived not from their action or consent but wholly from the command of the Act."[52] The RLA defined the term "representative" as "any person or . . . labor union . . . designated either by a carrier or group of carriers or by its or their employees, to act for it or them."[53] That definition "plainly implies that the representative is to act on behalf of all the employees which, by virtue of the statute, it undertakes to represent."[54] This reasoning supported the Court's finding that Congress did not intend to permit the unfair representation of minority workers. (As Congress knew about and did not prohibit union discrimination against black workers when it enacted and amended the RLA,[55] that finding is based on fictive legislative intent and is an exemplar of the Court's "legal gymnastics."[56])

Chief Justice Stone also focused on the purposes of the RLA, noting that the statute explicitly seeks to avoid interruptions of commerce and the operations of carriers.[57] "These purposes would hardly be attained if a substantial minority of the craft were denied the right to have their interests considered at the conference table and if the final result of the bargaining process were to be the sacrifice of the interests of the minority by the action of a representative chosen by the majority."[58] Minorities disadvantaged in this way could engage in strikes that would create the very interruption of commerce the RLA sought to avoid.

In addition, Chief Justice Stone found it significant that the RLA mandated that an employer bargain with the exclusive bargaining representative of a craft and with no other entity.[59] Given that statutory requirement, minority workers are deprived of the right to choose their own representatives and cannot engage in individual bargaining.[60] "The labor organization chosen to be the representative of the craft or class of employees is thus chosen to represent all of its members, regardless of their union affiliations or want of them."[61] Absent a legally enforceable union duty to represent and not discriminate against craft members, "the minority would be left with no means of protecting their interests, or indeed, their right to earn a livelihood by pursuing the occupation in which they are employed."[62] Thus, Chief Justice Stone wrote, the "fair interpretation of the statutory language is that the organization chosen to represent a craft is to represent all its members, the majority as well as the minority, and it is to act for and not against those whom it represents."[63] The RLA imposed on the union representative "at least as exacting a duty to protect equally the interests of the members of the craft as the Constitution imposes upon a legislature to give equal protection to the interests of those for whom it legislates."[64]

Answering in the affirmative the question posed at the beginning of the Court's opinion,[65] the Court declared: "We hold that the language of the Act to which we have referred, read in light of the purposes of the Act, expresses the aim of Congress to impose on the bargaining representative of a craft or class of employees the duty to exercise fairly the power conferred upon it in behalf of all those for whom it acts, without hostile discrimination against them."[66] While labor organizations are statutorily empowered to negotiate and agree to contract terms that vary based on relevant differences, that power "does not include the authority to make among members of the craft discriminations not based on such relevant differences. Here the discriminations based on race alone are obviously irrelevant and invidious. Congress plainly did not undertake to authorize the bargaining representative to make such discriminations."[67] The RLA "does require the union, in collective bargaining and in making contracts with the carrier, to represent nonunion or minority union members of the craft without hostile discrimination, fairly, impartially, and in good faith."[68] Accordingly, the Alabama Supreme Court's judgment was reversed and the case was remanded for further proceedings.

It is noteworthy that the *Steele* Court did not invalidate the Brotherhood's exclusion of African Americans from union membership, as the Court opined that the RLA "does not deny to such a bargaining labor organization the right to determine eligibility to its membership."[69] In a separate concurring opinion Justice Frank Murphy declaimed that the "cloak of racism surrounding the actions of the Brotherhood in refusing membership to Negroes and in entering into and enforcing agreements discriminating against them, all under the guise of Congressional authority, still remains. No statutory interpretation can erase this ugly example of economic cruelty against colored citizens of the United States."[70]

The *Steele* decision was an important development in labor law, civil rights, and employment discrimination law. The Court's creation of a union's duty "to represent non-union or minority union members of the craft without hostile discrimination, fairly, impartially, and in good faith"[71] imposed a legal obligation on the Brotherhood and other unions to "act for and not against those whom it represents"[72] and signaled that certain traditional and entrenched policies and customs targeting and subordinating black workers were no longer lawful.

Houston was pleased with the victory in *Steele* but was fully aware of the limits of the Court's decision.[73] As previously discussed, the Court did not outlaw the Brotherhood's racist exclusion of black workers from membership in the union. Professor Herbert Hill has noted "the lack of condemnation of the union's discriminatory membership practices" in the Court's opinion.[74]

> The exclusion of Negroes from membership effectively denied them notice of pending agreements or participation in the internal political affairs of the union and denied them a voice in the negotiating process. The doctrine of fair representation as thus interpreted was therefore tantamount to an application of the "separate but equal" doctrine. The union was allowed to treat Negroes as a separate class, excluded from

membership, but was expected to negotiate equally on their behalf. The Court was aware that the union's constitution contained a "white-only" membership clause and that the union adhered to it. By condoning such practices, the Court permitted them to continue.[75]

Houston also understood that *Steele* considered the rights of black workers who had obtained employment but did not address discriminatory practices and customs that excluded black jobseekers.[76]

Furthermore, many railroad unions continued their racist practices in the years following the Court's decision, and

> The promise *Steele* held for African Americans was not realized, because the relevant government agencies did not enforce it vigorously, and because private parties lacked the resources to litigate. Indeed, the discriminatory agreement that led to the *Steele* case remained in force until 1951. By the time *Steele* began to give African American railroad workers some leverage against discrimination in the 1950s, the bulk of African Americans' jobs on the railroads had been lost. For example, the presence of African American firemen in the South declined to only 7 percent in 1960. By the time railroad unions revoked their color bars in the 1960s, overall railroad employment had declined dramatically, and few railroads were doing much hiring.[77]

Recognition of the limits of the *Steele* decision should not obscure the jurisprudential impact of the Court's decision. *Steele* is the foundational precedent for the Court's fair representation canon[78] and the National Labor Relations Board's determination that a union's breach of its duty of fair representation is an unfair labor practice and violates the National Labor Relations Act.[79] The Court's decision and holding, announced ten years before *Brown v. Board of Education*,[80] gave voice to black workers who had long been subjected to rank and invidious discrimination. Bester William Steele, Charles Hamilton Houston, and all who challenged the conduct repudiated by the Court made a significant contribution to the antidiscrimination project. That contribution should and must be acknowledged and celebrated.

Notes

1. Alumnae Law Center Professor of Law, University of Houston Law Center. J.D., University of Pennsylvania Law School; B.A., Wilberforce University.
2. 323 U.S. 192 (1944).
3. 323 U.S. 214 (1944).
4. 347 U.S. 483 (1954).
5. 323 U.S. at 202–03; see also Tunstall v. Brotherhood of Locomotive Firemen and Enginemen, Local Lodge No. 76, 323 U.S. 210 (1944) (in companion case decided the same day as *Steele* the Court held that plaintiff's duty of fair representation claim against his union stated a cause of action); TIMOTHY J. BOYCE & RONALD TURNER, FAIR REPRESENTATION, THE NLRB AND THE COURTS

(rev. ed. 1984) (discussing the development and implications of the law of fair representation).

6. *See* Steele v. Louisville & Nashville Railroad. 16 So.2d 416. 417 (Ala. 1944), *rev'd,* 323 U.S. 192 (1944).
7. *Steele,* 323 U.S. at 194.
8. *Id.* at 195.
9. *See id.* at 195–96.
10. *Steele,* 16 So.2d at 417.
11. *Steele,* 323 U.S. at 196.
12. *Steele,* 323 U.S. at 196; *Steele,* 16 So.2d at 417.
13. *Steele,* 323 U.S. at 197.
14. *See* Deborah C. Malamud, *The Story of* Steele v. Louisville & Nashville *Railroad: White Unions, Black Unions, and the Struggle for Racial Justice on the Rails, in* LABOR LAW STORIES 75 (Laura J. Cooper & Catherine L. Fisk eds., 2005).
15. 45 U.S. C. § 151 *et seq.*
16. *Steele,* 16 So.2d at 418; see Virginian Ry. Co. v. System Federation, 300 U.S. 515, 545 (1937) (regarding the RLA and the employer's duty to bargain with the certified union representative: "It is, we think, not open to doubt that Congress intended that this requirement be mandatory upon the railroad employer. and that its command, in a proper case, be enforced by the courts.").
17. *See* 45 U. S. C. § 152, Fourth ("Employees shall have the right to organize and bargain collectively through representatives of their own choosing. The majority of any craft or class of employees shall have the right to determine who shall be the representative of the craft or class for the purposes of this chapter.").
18. *Steele,* 16 So.2d at 420.
19. *Id.* at 419.
20. *Id.*
21. *Id.*
22. *Id.*
23. *See supra* note 6 and accompanying text.
24. Cameron v. International Alliance of Theatrical Stage Emp.. 118 N. J. Eq. 11, 176 A. 692, 697 (1935).
25. Brotherhood of Railway and S.S. Clerks v. United Transport Service Employees of America, 137 F.2d 817. 821 (D.C. Cir. 1943). *judgment rev'd,* 320 U.S. 715 (1943).
26. *Steele,* 16 So.2d at 421.
27. *Id.* at 421–22.
28. 163 U.S. 537 (1896). For discussion and analysis of *Plessy.* see Ronald Turner, *Plessy 2.0,* 13 LEWIS & CLARK L. REV. 861 (2009).
29. *Steele,* 16 So.2d at 422.
30. Petition for Writ of Certiorari to the Supreme Court and Brief in Support Thereof (1944), at p. 11.
31. *Id.* at p. 14. Recall the Alabama Supreme Court's conclusion that Congress did not intend to create such a confidential relationship. *See supra* note 21 and accompanying text.
32. *See* Petition for Certiorari, *supra* note 29, at p. 4.
33. RICHARD A. POSNER, THE FEDERAL COURTS: CRISIS AND REFORM 286–87 (1985); see also Burnet v. Guggenheim. 288 U.S. 280, 285 (1933) (stating that a judge should ask "which choice is it the more likely that Congress would have made?").
34. *See* LARRY ALEXANDER & EMILY SHERWIN, THE RULE OF RULES: MORALITY, RULES, AND THE DILEMMAS OF LAW 119 (2001); WILLIAM N. ESKRIDGE, JR., DYNAMIC STATUTORY INTERPRETATION 16 (1994).

35. DAVID E. BERNSTEIN, ONLY ONE PLACE OF REDRESS: AFRICAN AMERICANS, LABOR REGULATIONS, AND THE COURTS FROM RECONSTRUCTION TO THE NEW DEAL 63 (2001).

36. *See* ESKRIDGE, *supra* note 33, at 26; see generally HENRY M. HART & ALBERT M. SACKS, THE LEGAL PROCESS: BASIC PROBLEMS IN THE MAKING AND APPLICATION OF LAW (William N. Eskridge & Philip P. Frickey eds., 1994) (advocating a purposivist approach in matters of statutory interpretation).

37. Peter L. Strauss, *The Common Law and Statutes*, 70 U. COLO. L. REV. 225, 227 (1999); see also STEPHEN BREYER, ACTIVE LIBERTY: INTERPRETING OUR DEMOCRATIC CONSTITUTION 85 (2005) (judges "should pay primary attention to a statute's purpose in difficult cases of interpretation in which language is not clear").

38. Ronald Turner, *On the Authority of the Two-Member NLRB: Statutory Interpretation Approaches and Judicial Choices*, 27 HOFSTRA LAB. & EMP. L. J. 13, 22 (2009).

39. *See* U.S. CONST. amend. V (1791) ("No person shall . . . be deprived of life, liberty, or property, without due process of law."). The petition conceded "that the restraints of the Fifth Amendment have not yet been applied to the actions of private individuals proceeding without reference to a grant of governmental authority." Petition for Writ of Certiorari, at p. 15.

40. Petition for Writ of Certiorari, at p. 16.

41. *Id.* at 17.

42. *Id.* at 20.

43. *See* Steele v. Louisville & N. R. Co., 322 U.S. 722 (1944).

44. *See* Malamud, *supra* note 13, at 85. As Professor Malamud has noted, references to a merits brief filing in *Steele* are made in J. Clay Smith, Jr. & E. Desmond Hogan, *Remembered Hero, Forgotten Contribution: Charles Hamilton Houston, Legal Realism, and Labor Law*, 14 HARV. BLACKLETTER L.J. 1, 9–10 (1998), and in Karl E. Klare, *The Quest for Industrial Democracy and the Struggle Against Racism: Perspectives from Labor Law and Civil Rights Law*, 61 OR. L. REV. 157, 189 n.127 (1982). Malamud reports that "[m]onths after the Court granted review, Houston confided to Shores that he had not yet written the brief on the merits in *Steele* . . . he confidently stated that 'we can stand on our brief supporting the petition for certiorari.'" Malamud, *supra* note 13, at 85. Further support for the conclusion that a merits brief was not filed is found in the Louisville & Nashville Railroad Company's brief to the Supreme Court: "At the time of the preparation of this brief, the Respondent . . . has not been served, and is without [the] brief of petitioner on the merits." Brief for Louisville & Nashville Railroad Company (Nov. 1944), at p.1.

45. Malamud, *supra* note 13, at 88.

46. *Id.* at 89 (quoting Douglas).

47. Steele v. Louisville & N. R. Co., 323 U.S. 192 (1944).

48. *Id.* at 198–99.

49. In a concurring opinion Justice Frank Murphy argued that the "economic discrimination against Negroes practiced by the Brotherhood and the railroad under the color of Congressional authority raises a grave constitutional issue that should be squarely faced." *Id.* at 208 (Murphy, J., concurring). Not willing to assume that Congress meant to authorize the union to ignore constitutional rights—"[o]therwise the Act would bear the stigma of unconstitutionality under the Fifth Amendment"—he was "willing to read the statute as not permitting or allowing any action" by a union that would violate an individual's constitutional rights. *Id.* at 208–09.

50. *Id.* at 199.

51. *See supra* note 6 and accompanying text.

52. 323 U.S. at 199.

53. 45 U.S. C. § 151, Sixth.

54. 323 U.S. at 199.
55. *See supra* note 34 and accompanying text.
56. BERNSTEIN, *supra* note 34, at 63; see also Karl E. Klare, *Traditional Labor Law Scholarship and the Crisis of Collective Bargaining Law: A Reply to Professor Finkin*, 44 MD. L. REV. 731, 788 (1985) ("The *Steele* Court's holding that Congress intended a duty of fair representation, even one that, as in *Steele* still allowed unions to continue their whites-only membership policy, is questionable.").
57. *See id.*; 45 U.S. C. § 152, First.
58. 323 U.S. at 200.
59. *See* 45 U. S. C. § 152, Second.
60. *See* 323 U.S. at 200; Order of Railroad Telegraphers v. Railway Express Agency, 321 U.S. 342 (1944). *See also* J. I. Case Co. v NLRB, 321 U.S. 332 (1944) ("Individual contracts, no matter what the circumstances that justify their execution or what their terms, may not be availed of to defeat or delay the procedures prescribed by the National Labor Relations Act looking to collective bargaining . . . nor may they be used to forestall bargaining or to limit or condition the terms of the collective agreement.").
61. 323 U.S. at 200.
62. *Id.* at 201.
63. *Id.* at 202.
64. *Id.*; see also *id.* ("Congress has seen fit to clothe the bargaining representative with powers comparable to those possessed by a legislative body both to create and restrict the rights of those whom it represents."). For an extended discussion of this aspect of the Court's decision, see Michael C. Harper & Ira C. Lupu, *Fair Representation as Equal Protection*, 98 HARV. L. REV. 1211 (1985).
65. *See supra* note 46 and accompanying text.
66. 323 U.S. at 202–03.
67. *Id.* at 203.
68. *Id.* at 204.
69. *Id.*
70. *Id.* at 209 (Murphy, J., concurring).
71. *Steele*, 323 U.S. at 204.
72. *Id.* at 202.
73. *See* GENNA RAE MCNEIL, GROUNDWORK: CHARLES HAMILTON HOUS-TON AND THE STRUGGLE FOR CIVIL RIGHTS 169–71 (1983).
74. HERBERT HILL, BLACK LABOR AND THE AMERICAN LEGAL SYSTEM: RACE, WORK, AND THE LAW 110 (1985).
75. *Id.*
76. *See* MCNEIL, *supra* note 72, at 171.
77. BERNSTEIN, *supra* note 34, at 64 (footnotes omitted). As noted in the text, the collective bargaining agreement challenged in *Steele* was operative until the parties reached a settlement in November 1951. *See* Malamud, *supra* note 13, at 100. Houston died in 1950 before the settlement was reached; Bester William Steele died in February 1954. *Id.* at 99, 100.
78. *See, e.g.*, Air Line Pilots Association v. O'Neill, 499 U.S. 65 (1991); United Steelworkers of America v. Rawson, 495 U.S. 362 (1990); Vaca v. Sipes, 386 U.S. 171 (1967); Conley v. Gibson, 355 U.S. 41 (1957); Ford Motor Co. v. Huffman, 345 U.S. 330 (1953); Graham v. Brotherhood of Locomotive Firemen & Enginemen, 338 U.S. 232 (1949).
79. *See* Miranda Fuel Co., 140 N. L. R. B. 181 (1962), *enforced*, 284 F.2d 861 (2d Cir. 1960), *judgment vacated*, 366 U. S. 763 (1961).
80. 347 U. S. 483 (1954).

9

Our Fate or Our Future:
The Hip Hop Nation and Alternative
Intentional Communities for Social Justice

"Our youth can be our fate or our future." —Maulana Karenga
"Anything we love can be saved." —Alice Walker
"The world is yours to change." —Daisaku Ikeda

Lisbeth Gant-Britton

Introduction

As we witness the global capitalist economic system slowly erode before
our very eyes, taking many of our long-cherished opportunities with it,
important questions come to mind. One is, what are the ways in which
we, particularly middle- and working-class people of African descent,
"make community" to make change? As Avery Gordon notes, "We are not
confronted simply or only by individual anxieties or problems. We face
social problems requiring public and collective solutions (16). A dozen
years into the new century, I ask myself, do we still perceive how much
we need each other to get such a big job done or how much we need our
young? I remind myself and anyone else who will listen about the ways
we historically came together in this country around communities formed
purely in our minds because those imagined spaces were the only places
we initially had. They eventually became what some scholars now call

"intentional communities." One way to think of it is that we were so intent on our goals we simply wouldn't give them up until they existed in lived reality rather than in our heads.

What visions do we have *now* of a fundamentally better future or futures? And how do we share them with one another these days? How are we inspiring each other and, most importantly, our young? As Robin D.G. Kelley has observed, "Without new visions we don't know what to build, only what to knock down. We not only end up confused, rudderless, and cynical, but we forget that making a revolution is not a series of clever maneuvers and tactics but a process that can and must transform us" (xii).

I wanted to find the new contemporary intentional communities of color that were already out there making change. As Alain Touraine suggests, "What is true at the individual level is also true at the collective level. We want to find complex beings who combine the present with the past, and their heritage with new interventions" (197). I wanted to see if, outside of a few broad coalitions like BAMN (By Any Means Necessary) and the Occupy Movement, there were at least a few new social justice intentional communities populated by people of African descent, particularly young people. Did they have a strong sense of unity and shared purpose? And were they already tackling the transformation of some of these thorny sociocultural issues? My research assistant and I started to search. We unearthed a precious few new intentional communities of color amid the cracks and crevices of a severely battered social justice movement. The tiny, embryonic collectivities we found share either real places or imaged spaces. But if one looks hard enough, each can be considered an all-important seed ready to sprout. Together, their emergence could well lead to the reemergence of a broader collective national social justice framework for all people of color and other colleagues of good conscience in the future. And not a moment too soon.

Intentional Communities, Then and Now

The term "intentional communities" has not often been used regarding African American sociocultural movements up to now. In order to examine these budding new intentional communities and their potential future impact for people of African descent in the US, it is important first to take a brief look at what intentional communities are and how they have developed here. Intentional communities fall into two broad categories. The first includes those whose adherents have a strongly shared ("public service") vision, life philosophy, or social stance. The second involves people who actually reside ("homestead") together based on a common belief system rather than accidental occupancy. As Lisa Paulson, who has lived in a Wisconsin eco-village called High Wind for over fourteen years, describes it, "Within the term intentional community, we make two distinctions: 'public' or 'homesteading.' Public intentional communities are dedicated to public service, outreach, educational programs, events, and networking. Such groups are broad, even global, in scope. . . . [Homesteading is] a group of people who come together deliberately in a residential situation around a specific vision, agenda or shared values".[1] Given the growing difficulty, for instance, for people of color with limited financial means and retirees on fixed incomes to purchase single-family homes, this intentional community movement could become an important model of a new kind of communitarian self-empowerment. Although it is almost impossible to ascertain accurate figures, experts estimate there are thousands of groups living together in some kind of intentional communities in the United States and internationally.[2]

Historically, people of African descent, by necessity, had to create and use intentional communities almost from the moment we were forcibly brought to the New World. Ripped from our homelands and families and thrown together with other captives whose languages we frequently couldn't speak and cultures we didn't understand, almost immediately we had to devise new ways to reimagine family and community. Soon thereafter, we took our new imagined communities even a step further. We created clandestine intentional communities as imaginary spaces in which to secretly nurture our shared visions of freedom so they couldn't be taken away. Only in our collective imaginary could they incubate safely until they could finally give birth to actual events: slave escapes and revolts in which the participants' shared visions of the future became real.[3]

Fast forward to the Civil Rights movement in which Dr. King invoked imagery of a spiritual intentional community in an attempt to share his vision of inclusiveness. He referred to the nineteenth-century reformer Josiah Royce's idea of a "beloved community." As David Levering Lewis notes of Dr. King, "He summoned the politically weak, the economically deprived, the angry young of all races, and the antiwar liberals to form together a community of action sufficiently powerful to force the enlightened attention of Washington and Wall Street. . . . [He would] begin to create the Beloved Community" (19). Further, Hanes Walton refers to Dr. King's effort to "reestablish the wholeness of community, reconcile the oppressor with the oppressed and create a brotherhood of blacks and whites," in the creation of the "beloved community" (190).

That beloved community would not have much time to blossom before war would break out again. And the late 1960s would witness a powerful reaction to it in the form of the Anti-Vietnam War movement. But as a 2005 documentary entitled *Sir! No Sir!* explains, this GI movement, as it loosely became known, actually began as an intentional community. It included many inspirational African Americans soldiers such as Greg Payton, imprisoned for his refusal to fight against other people of color. At first, this intentional community was the only way the GIs could hold onto their collective antiwar dream. Then gradually it grew into a massive social protest movement in lived reality that eventually spurred the war's end. As the documentary's producer/director, David Zeiger, asserts:

> In the course of a few short years, over 100 underground newspapers were published by soldiers around the world; local and national antiwar GI organizations were joined by thousands; thousands more demonstrated against the war at every major base in the world in 1970 and 1971, *including* in Vietnam itself; stockades and federal prisons were filling up with soldiers jailed for their opposition to the war and the military.

The film's closing credits and song, "Captain Sterling's Little Problem,"[4] are sung by the radically political Oakland hip hop social justice collective, The Coup, which is part of one of the country's embryonic new intentional communities.

Ever since the sixties, theorists of color have continued to call for mutually empowering ways in which to share visions of new spaces and places in which fresh productive forms of social interaction could take hold. In *Methodologies of the Oppressed*, Chela Sandoval calls for "a redefined 'decolonizing theory and method' that can better prepare us for a radical turn during the new millennium, when the utopian dreams inherent in an internationalist, egalitarian, non-oppressive, socialist-feminist democracy can take their place in the real" (5). Each time I read about Sandoval's ideal, I think of the often grueling real-life challenges many of us face, not the least of whom are my students. On the one hand, their world, with its overlapping and intersecting gendered, political, and socioeconomic interactions, seems wider, more global, than ever before. But on the other hand, many are faced with narrower future prospects than ever before, defined by a shrinking global economy and a media-saturated society that make it hard for youth of African descent to avoid blurring boundaries between fact and fantasy as they try to focus on the future. But in spite of this, I am happy to see small numbers of socially conscious youth of African descent breaking free. Indeed, many are developing micro-level alternative groups and collectives within one of the largest contemporary intentional communities the world has ever seen: the Hip Hop Nation.

The Hip Hop Nation as an Intentional Community

Now that hip hop has been around for a generation, it has achieved the status of an intentional community itself. Despite many sharp distinctions and disagreements between members in sociocultural change, the term still invokes a shared ethos with a range of common visions, philosophies, rituals, and traditions. As A.K. Asante, Jr. asserts in *It's Bigger Than Hip Hop*, "When we consider hip hop's origins and purpose, we understand it is a revolutionary cultural force that was intended to challenge the status quo and the greater American culture. So its relegation to reflecting American culture becomes extremely problematic if one considers the radical tradition of African-American social movements—which have never been about mirroring dominant American culture." (8)

In terms of shared places, hip hop has reached iconic status there too. It now has its own pilgrimage venues. West Coast tourists frequently visit Compton and Watts and East Coast tourists now regularly make pilgrimages to sites in Manhattan, Harlem, and Brooklyn. As Julia Chance noted in a recent blog on TheRoot.com:

> "A quick group photo in front of Yankee Stadium was followed by what I consider the pilgrimage part of the tour: a visit to the apartment building at 1520 Sedgwick Avenue, where, on August 11, 1973, in a rec-room party for his sister, 16-year-old Clive Campbell, later known as DJ Kool Herc, debuted a new deejaying style that would become the foundation of hip-hop's sound."[5]

From those early origins to the multimillion dollar global industry it is today, hip hop has matured into two oppositional camps: consumerist party music and social justice rhymes.

Hip Hop: Spawning Embryonic Social Justice Intentional Communities

As Bakari Kitwana and others observe, hip hop began as a small, disjointed, fragmented counter-culture movement that gradually grew and coalesced into more cohesive, although frequently argumentative, collectives. For nearly a generation, within the larger hip hop community, very small numbers of socially conscious MCs and spoken word artists gradually began to emerge. This early wing had a firm social vision. They were on their way to becoming a smaller, more radically focused intentional community within the larger national and international hip hop world. Evelyn Higginbotham points to "[g]roups such as A Tribe Called Quest, De La Soul, and Leaders of the New School, all affiliated with the Native Tongues and Zulu Nation collectives, [who] brought to the music an eclectic mix of black-nationalist rhetoric and New Age spirituality that came to define a socially 'conscious' sound" (604).

Alternative music MC Dead Prez have created songs that literally teach while they sing, almost as if they were teachers in an alternative intentional community. In "Be Healthy" they counsel:

Lentil soup is mental fruit
And ginger root is good for the yout'
Fresh veg-e-table with the mayatl stew
Sweet yam fries with the green calalloo
Careful how you season and prepare your foods
Cause you don't wanna lose vitamins and miner-ules
And that's the jewel
Life brings life, it's valuable, so I eat what comes
From the ground, it's natural
Let your food be your medicine (uh huh)
No Excedrin (uh uh)
Strictly herb, generate in the sun, cause I got melanin
And drink water, eight glasses a day
Cause that's what they say[6]

With more African American youth being inspired by hip hop than health warnings, in spite of the fact that 21 percent of them are more likely to be overweight than their white counterparts,[7] the above lyrics are a good example of how this genre can function as an empowering intentional community if socially conscious MCs can continue to stay focused on their mission more than on money.

Dead Prez would eventually be joined by the likes of Yasiin Bey (formerly Mos Def) and Talib Kweli (known collectively as Black Star since the 1990s), who see hip hop as an opportunity to "drop science" and turn listeners on to knowledge they may not have gotten in school, including black history. Thus the name of their collective, Black Star, refers to Marcus Garvey's Black Star Line. It gestures back to one of the most famous (and infamous) black intentional communities in history, the United Negro Improvement Association (UNIA), founded in 1914. Brainchild of early black nationalist leader, Marcus Garvey, the self-help oriented UNIA gathered funds from poor and working-class black people and attempted to establish businesses and found organizations that ideally would have created sustainable, more self-reliant futures for masses of the working poor.

By invoking the name Black Star, these hip hop artists inspired themselves and their youthful audiences, many of whom had never clearly understood the significance of the historic, although ill-fated, Garvey organization and its potential economic and sociopolitical sweep. In one fell swoop, these contemporary youth and their young audiences yoked themselves imaginatively to the largest twentieth-century black intentional community ever to exist. Bey and Kweli thus created a late twentieth-century imaginary association with an early twentieth-century intentional community that actually existed. In so doing, they have attempted to instill in the minds of an entire new generation the possibility that such a vastly ambitious undertaking could happen again, perhaps this time with more lasting success. If it happened once, why not again? Bey and Kweli are models of alternative intentionality. They continued to make their own music in the face of corporate-sponsored mega productions, to provoke more youth to think. Might an intentional community gradually emerge of youth who decide to "fix up" and "look up" like the early abolitionists and Civil Rights activists before them?

We can look back and see that those early Civil Rights groups also fashioned intentional communities to be able to hang onto the radical sociocultural ideas they had. Initially, their ideas could only exist in their minds. And often, it was the poets, musicians, and spoken word artists who helped them hang on with lyrics like "We Shall Overcome." Is it important that the artists kept the intentions alive? As Robin D. G. Kelley reflects, it sure is.

> Sometimes I think the conditions of daily life, of everyday oppressions, of survival, not to mention the temporary pleasures accessible to most of us, render much of our imagination inert. We are constantly putting out fires, responding to emergencies, finding temporary refuge, all of which makes it difficult to see anything other than the present. . . . When movements have been unable to clear the clouds, it has been the poets—no matter the medium—who have succeeded in imagining the color of the sky, in rendering the kinds of dreams and futures social movements are capable of producing (11).

As Kelley suggests, the spoken word artists among us can play important roles in helping us keep on keepin' on. They can help us hold our ideas tightly. They can envision and help us build imaginary girders until we have real tools to keep our embryonic social structures in place.

As Bey (Mos Def) and Kweli and Black Star do, by "dropping science" and including history in their music, they allow youth of African descent to "sample" older models of early bold African American social justice ventures and incorporate into their contemporary lives. In their song, "K. O. S. (Determination)," Black Star attempts to rekindle dormant political attitudes in their youthful listeners:

> So many emcees focusin' on black people extermination
> We keep it balanced with knowledge of self, determination
> It's hot, we be blowin' the spots, with conversations
> C'mon let's smooth it out like Soul Sensation
> We in the house like Japanese in Japan, or Koreans in Korea
> Head to Philly and free Mumia with the Kujichagulia TRUE
> Singin' is swingin' and writin' is fightin', but what
> they writin' got us clashin' like titans it's not exciting
> No question, bein' a black man is demandin'
> The fire's in my eyes and the flames need fannin'
> With what? (Knowledge of self) Determination.[8]

The rhymes speak forcefully of self-empowerment. And with African American communities facing the sobering fact that young black males are outnumbered two to one in college by their female counterparts,[9] music such as this is sorely needed. It helps engender a strong sense of productive intentionality in our young black men that may in turn allow them to focus on social justice, community, and personal empowerment rather than consumerism or crime.

Today, a tiny number of new socially conscious hip hop artists joins their elder counterparts. They, too, are focused on sociocultural critique more than on cash back. As these tiny groups pop up here and there, they add to the small but growing counterculture hip hop intentional community. Very slowly, it grows, but grow it does, hopefully to swell imperceptibly until it becomes a critical mass of global proportions—a full-blown, global, socially conscious intentional community more interested in uniting than blinging.[10]

MapQuesting for Mini-Social Justice Intentional Communities of Color

If we click our cursor on Oakland, California, original home of Huey P. Newton's Black Panthers of the 1960s, we discover that a tiny socially conscious hip hop collective known as Hieroglyphics has emerged these days. Members have a spectrum of political views, from optimistic and hopeful to more scathing critiques. One of them, Pep Love, muses:

> As our economy continues to decay, it's strange that mainstream hip-hop grows more ostentatious and flashy, whispering into our ears of what we still don't have. What's more perplexing is that we listen to these sensational verses preaching to us about fortune and sex as we go through our persistently ordinary routines of morning commutes, lines at the post office and walks between classes. The ideal image of success is envisioned for us by those who become less relatable by the verse—and little to nothing is being lyricized about the rough, rocky road that lies between us and that reverie.[11]

The title of Pep Love's latest compilation is *Rigmarole*. With lyrics like "got this lint in my pocket/plus my landlord knocking at my door/ whatever he wants/I don't got it," Pep Love imaginatively joins shoulder to shoulder with his beleaguered listeners in imagined solidarity and community.

Another more radically political group loosely associated with Oakland's growing social justice intentional communities is The Coup, a tiny hip hop collective headed by MC Raymond "Boots" Riley. As Eric Arnold of the *East Bay Express* notes, at just nineteen, Riley and others formed the Mau Mau Rhythm Collective in 1991. Instead of performing party music, they gave "consciousness-raising edutainment," much like Black Star's "dropping science." Then Riley started The Coup in 1992, taking its name from the term *coup d'état*, which means a radical overthrow of a government. One of The Coup's most popular albums was the 1998 *Steal This Album*, a take-off on the white political rebel Abbie Hoffman's 1971 written volume entitled *Steal This Book*. Riley has spent years as a social activist in the Oakland area and in 2011 briefly joined the Occupy Movement. One way he speaks out in favor of his brand of intentionality is to advocate for his version of communism, which stresses "people having democratic control over the profits that they create."[12] To prove their point, Riley and his Coup partners operate as, and with, independent producers.

Taking It to the Streets: Homesteading Intentional Communities of Color

One of the most committed forms of intentional communities is homesteading, where adherents actually live together under mutually agreed upon rules and in mutually constructive living conditions. Historically, as far back as the colonial era, many early African Americans shared a dream of escaping to freedom and homesteading on their own. The late nineteenth and early twentieth centuries saw intrepid black freedmen and women actually strike out to settle all-black towns. Many of these early communities perished, but a few remain, if only as historic sites. Just north of Bakersfield, California, now a California State Park, are the remains of the town of Allensworth, the most famous early all-black community in the state. It was founded in 1908 by Colonel Allen Allensworth, former slave and Civil War veteran and just four other settlers. "Their dream of developing an abundant and thriving community stemmed directly from a strong belief in programs that allowed blacks to help themselves create better lives."[13]

Meanwhile, Eatonville, Florida, originally an all-black town and still majority black, exists today. One of the earliest African American villages, it was incorporated in 1887. It was made famous by Harlem Renaissance writer, Zora Neale Hurston who grew up there. She fictionalized its origins in her well-known novel, *Their Eyes Were Watching God.* Early audiences thrilled vicariously to the thought of the tiny community making its own decisions. Even today, the real Eatonville hosts an annual Zora Neale Hurston festival. It is a reminder that, at first, the dream of such an all-black municipality existed only as an imagined intentional community. But its adherents held fast, purchased land, and worked cooperatively and eventually the actual town came into existence.[14]

Later in the twentieth century, large northern urban municipalities emerged with substantial populations of color. Even though their entire cities were not black, a shared intention toward productive decision-making among many African Americans and other people of color held sway. For instance, in 1972, under the leadership of black mayor Richard G. Hatcher and other civil rights figures, Gary, Indiana would be the site of the first Black National Convention. Although its historic conference lasted only a few days, overall, the collective endeavor can be considered a mid-twentieth-century imagined intentional community. And that is because the convention was the end-product of a decades-old, tightly guarded, shared array of visions of black community. Its manifesto, The National Black Political Agenda, declares, "At every critical moment of our struggle in America we have had to press relentlessly against the limits of the 'realistic' to create new realities for the life of our people. This is our challenge at Gary and beyond, for a new Black politics demands new vision, new hope and new definitions of the possible. Our time has come. These things are necessary. All things are possible."[15] These shared ideals still resonate today. Nowadays, we may take black mayors and governors of large urban areas for granted. But it bears remembering that not two generations ago, such a thing was still a dream, one that had to be carefully nurtured and doggedly developed in imagined intentional communities before becoming a reality. Kitwana, following older critics like Kalamu Ya Salaam, has called for a "working united front" of youthful activists, financed in part by artists such as wealthy young hip hop moguls. They could, as Kitwana notes, "greatly enhance rap's potential to contribute to needed sociopolitical transformations." He adds, "All the components for a mass political movement in our lifetime are in place and functioning—but separate. Do we dare join them together" (215)?

At the same time that youthful activists contemplate joining together intellectually and politically, others are joining together in actual living spaces. Young people of color are beginning to experiment with residential intentional communities. Cohousing and shared living that is controlled by people of color, young and old alike, is just in its infant stages. But many are realizing that the individualistic single-family "American Dream" lifestyle is rapidly becoming the Great American nightmare. Currently, a smattering of alternative residential modes of living for people of color has begun to emerge. These range from cohousing arrangements to shared apartment buildings and co-ops to eco-villages and even group farms. Going back to our Oakland, California, model, one example of intentional residential living is an apartment building currently being shared by six families. As they put it on their website:

> Six of us live in intentional spiritual community at 1724 Filbert Street in West Oakland, trying to be good neighbors and seeking to be transformed by our interactions with each other, with our neighbors, and with the Spirit of Life (which we understand in various ways, and very imperfectly). We are a kind of "halfway house" for people in recovery from classism; racism; internalized oppression; addictions to status, work, and perfection; and other aspects of the dominant culture that separate us from each other and limit our aliveness.[16]

This six-family cohort is part of a larger intentional community—The West Oakland Reconciliation & Social Healing Project. It is attempting to forge the residents of this larger urban space into more of a cohesive unit by way of a project they call The Seminary of the Street. As its website declares,

> At Seminary of the Street, we believe with Martin Luther King, Jr., that "no one is free until everyone is free," and we are wondering whether our gentrifying neighborhoods, where people of different races, ethnicities, and income levels are living side by side, might be a place to begin exploring what real freedom would look like.[17]

The Seminary of the Street sees itself as training "love warriors working toward the transformation of their communities." As one 2012 participant,

Gillian Siple, blogged, "Come be in a supportive community with whatever burdens you hold, with all your vulnerability and self-doubt, even self-hate, and be in a place of love and authenticity."[18]

While West Oakland is a good example of an urban intentional community; at the other end of the spectrum are the still-embryonic efforts of a few black farm collectives. The most notable may well be that of the Nation of Islam. They have created a collective called the Center for Intentional and Communal Development that urges black people to purchase and manage farmland for greater independence. As the NOI asserts, quoting its founder, The Honorable Elijah Muhammad,

> In order to be recognized today you must represent your nation. We must understand the importance of land of our own. The first and most important reason that the individual countries of Europe, Africa and Asia are recognized as nations is because they occupy a specific area of the earth. Second, they are recognized because of the effectiveness of their internal unity and policies and then by their enactment of international policies and agreements with other established nations. The black man has been actually worthless when it comes to exercising the rights as human beings in an ever-advancing civilization. So remember, we cannot demand recognition until we have some land that we can call our own.[19]

Thus, the NOI model may be one example of a trend that could eventually develop among other black religious institutions. To date, most, like Los Angeles's mega-churches, have already begun to acquire property to support their practitioners' economic as well as spiritual needs.

Where Do We Go from Here? Imagining
Empowered Futures through Fiction

How to refresh and restock our imaginations to conceive of new intentional communities not only inhabited by people of color but actively influenced by them? One way is to examine fictional texts by Afrofuturist writers of color. They share a determination with black activists to create imaginative works that fill the gap between a seemingly impotent present and more ideal future. As Avery Gordon notes, "Science fiction scenarios are happening now and toward a future within very powerful institutions. These scenarios are about how power will be deployed and received. And, finally, questions about how language operates are crucial if we are committed to producing a counterdiscourse, if we intend to speak and write with the aim of social transformation" (97).

For example, Octavia Butler's novels *Parable of the Sower* and *Parable of the Talents* are set in the mid- to late-twenty-first-century America, which after generations of seeming prosperity, is at the brink of moral and economic bankruptcy. The future generation in the novel is paying the price for our excesses. Formerly middle-class citizens have to learn to live and work together in more cooperative ways because the resources for single-family homes, personal cars, and possessions have largely been exhausted. The novels contain perfect examples of tiny intentional communities that manage to empower themselves under the most difficult conditions. One small group creates a small intentional farming collective. Later it evolves into a national spiritual movement with its own compelling life philosophy, which the protagonist calls Earthseed, and large shared cooperative living spaces and communities. If one reads between the lines, the text is essentially a handbook of how this could be done.

The members of the makeshift intentional communities try to live together across lines of race, class, and gender. They barter and trade with one another. The young protagonist Lauren Olamina, endowed with a strong sense of empathy, eventually creates her Earthseed philosophy as one way toward a more workable level of cooperation and interaction. It is tenuously held together only in the minds of the small initial group of adherents. Then, years later, after it expands tremendously, it becomes the blueprint for many residential and educational communities. As Lucy Sargisson observes in *Dark Horizons*, "This may not be changing the world with dramatic and easily observable impact but it is, I think, what's required for sustainable and enduring transformation. This is a pluralist utopianism, and it's a utopianism of process. It's empowering in the now and isn't dependent on escapism or distant wish fulfillment, and it takes the way that we think as an essential part of social change" (18).

There is also a great need for social change in Walter Mosley's *Futureland* in which identity for all citizens is mediated by computerized corporate structures and devices. The novel includes characters that are made to have electronic devices implanted within their bodies that alter the ways in which they can relate to their lived reality. A "phono chip" is implanted in their brains, so the characters no longer actually "read" books or papers in a traditional sense. The phono chip reads *to* them, rendering them more passive. Thus, in consuming reading material, the power relationship is changed. The voice reading to the listener may subtly or drastically alter meaning. While this fictional device may seem ahead of its time, the recent development in our own time of e-books, Kindle readers, audiobooks, and soon Google glasses with embedded cameras and other electronic devices[20] has already made an impact, both positive and negative, on citizens', particularly youths', ability to communicate face to face, to gather together, make community, and make productive societal changes.

As more youth turn to popular culture and electronic commodities for validation, they frequently get a psychological boost from association with their certain products or fictional characters. But if we're not careful, terrible negative effects can also occur. One can lose his or her ability to rationally discern imagined communities from the real. Such was apparently the case with the alienated PhD student dropout who, on July 23, 2012, embarked on a shooting rampage in a Colorado movie theater. As if he were a character in the Batman *Dark Knight* film, he donned garments modeled after the villain. But then he actually mowed down real people.

In *Futureland*, Mosley posits a group of youth who, although surrounded by technology as never before, are not completed seduced by it. Instead, they create a secret intentional community to outmaneuver the massive computers that run everything in their futuristic world. This multiracial, multiethnic collective gestures to the kind of intelligence the author suggests youth will need in order to solve future problems in the information age. It will no longer be sufficient to leap tall buildings in a single bound. One will have to outthink the competition as well as outrun them. By depicting multiracial heroes who develop their brain power rather than brawn, Mosley subtly suggests that today's hip hop youth need to stay in school and become more than just nominally educated. If they really want to become effective, they will need to value education much more, not less. Mosley's small revolutionary intentional community is a fitting counterpart to much of the vacuous global corporate hip hop culture of today that is anything but intentional except intent on making a profit.

As Mosley and other Afrofuturist thinkers suggest, in order to make change to improve society, we have to start where we are and start small but keep our intent strong to make healthier, more empowered communities that can really make change. As he asserts in *What Next*, "I do not believe we can change the will of our government without first coming together in smaller organizations that are external to the recognized political systems. . . . Forget the large scale. Forget the proxies. What we need is each other and the recognition between us that all that peace is within our reach" (103, 105). As Mosley and Butler argue in both of their powerful works, for middle- and working-class people of African descent, it is imperative that we seize the initiative to visualize and craft the kind of future we want to live in right now in small, bite-sized pieces. Not to do so, to remain inactive, is NOT going to work because inaction will never make us safe.

Notes

1. "Definition of Intentional Communities, Shared Purpose, and Homesteading." *Fellowship for Intentional Community*. Lisa Paulson of High Wind eco-village in Intentional Communities Magazine. http://www.ic.org/pnp/cdir/1995/05quest.php.
2. "Intentional Communities: Lifestyles Based on Ideals." George Kozeny of Community Catalyst Project, San Francisco, California. http://www.ic.org/pnp/cdir/1995/01kozeny.php.
3. For a more general description of imagined communities, see also Benedict Anderson's *Imagined Communities: Reflections on the Origin and Spread of Nationalism*.
4. http://www.myspace.com/thecoupmusic.
5. The Root.com. http://www.theroot.com/.
6. Dead Prez, "Be Healthy" lyrics: http://www.elyrics.net/read/d/dead-prez-lyrics/be-healthy-lyrics.html.
7. U.S. Department of Health and Human Services. National Health and Nutrition Examination Survey (NHANES) found that African American and Mexican American adolescents ages 12–19 were more likely to be overweight, at 21 percent and 23 percent respectively, than non-Hispanic White adolescents (14 percent). http://aspe.hhs.gov/health/reports/child_obesity/.
8. Black Star, K.O.S. "Determination" lyrics: http://www.sing365.com/music/lyric.nsf/K-O-S-Determination-lyrics-Black-Star/A4D1D2DE2F63C9AF48256A17000FE183.
9. Black women enroll in college and earn bachelor's and master's degrees two times more often than black men. Student African American Brotherhood. http://saabnational.org/education.htm.
10. Black Star (Kweli and Bey) appeared on *The Colbert Report* on October 5, 2011, where they discussed not being aligned with a corporate music company but rather preferring to be independent.
11. Hieroglyphics Imperium. Oakland, California. http://www.hieroglyphics.com/. Pep Love.
12. Currently, the only site for this quote is Wikipedia. http://en.wikipedia.org/wiki/The_Coup.
13. California Department of Parks and Recreation. http://www.parks.ca.gov/?page_id=583.
14. http://www.zoranealehurstonfestival.com/.
15. Eyes on the Prize: America's Civil Rights Movement, 1954–1985. http://www.pbs.org/wgbh/amex/eyesontheprize/milestones/m13_nbpc.html.
16. Victor Lewis, Seminary of the Street, West Oakland Reconciliation & Social Healing Project. http://seminaryofthestreet.org/id27.html.
17. Seminary of the Street. NoOneFreeUntilEveryone.jpg. www.seminaryofthestreet.org/.
18. www.seminaryofthestreet.org/.
19. The Nation of Islam's Center for Intentional and Communal Development urges black people to purchase and manage farm land for greater independence. http://www.seventhfam.com/intentionalcommunity/.
20. Google Glasses. TechEye.net. http://news.techeye.net/hardware/google-s-project-glass-to-push-wearable-electronics-boom.

References

Anderson, Benedict. *Imagined Communities: Reflections on the Origin and Spread of Nationalism*. London: Verso, 2006.

Asante, M.K. *It's Bigger Than Hip Hop: The Rise of the Post-Hip-Hop Generation*. New York: St. Martin's Griffin, 2009.

Baccolini, Raffaella and Tom Moylan, eds. *Dark Horizons: Science Fiction and the Dystopian Imagination*. New York: Routledge, 2003.

Butler, Octavia. *Parable of the Sower*. New York: Grand Central Publishing, 2000.

———. *Parable of the Talents*. New York: Grand Central Publishing, 2000.

Chance, Julia. "Touring the City Where Hip-Hop Started: Explore the Roots of Rap and Graffiti on These Excursions Through New York's Boroughs." *The Root.com*. Last modified July 16, 2012, accessed July 17, 2012.

Colbert, Steven. *The Colbert Report*. Last modified 5 October 2011, accessed August 8, 2012. <http://www.colbertnation.com/the-colbert-report-videos/399066/october-05-2011/talib-kweli---yasiin-bey--a-k-a--mos-def>.

Davis, Mike. *City of Quartz: Excavating the Future in Los Angeles*. London: Verso, 2006.

Dead Prez. "Be Healthy." *YouTube*. Last modified December 9, 2007, accessed August 8, 2012. www.youtube.com/watch?v=YTAhSJt_8x8.

Higginbotham, Evelyn. *From Slavery to Freedom: A History of African Americans*. 9th ed. New York: McGraw-Hill, 2011.

Hurston, Zora Neale. *Their Eyes Were Watching God*. New York: HarperCollins, 1990. First published 1937.

Ikeda, Daisaku. *The World Is Yours to Change*. Sonoma, CA: Dunhill, 2004.

Islam, Nation of. "Intentional Community." *The Center for Intentional and Communal Development*. 2000. accessed August 8, 2012. http://www.seventhfam.com/intentionalcommunity/.

Karenga, Maulana. "Interview from *The Source*," in *The Hip Hop Generation: Young Blacks and the Crisis in African American Culture*, Bakari Kitwana. New York: Basic Civitas Books, 2002.

Kelley, Robin D. G. *Freedom Dreams*. Boston: Beacon Press, 2003.

Kitwana, Bakari. *The Hip Hop Nation: Young Blacks and the Crisis in African American Culture*. New York: Basic Civitas Books, 2002.

Kozeny, George. "Intentional Communities: Lifestyles Based on Ideals," *Fellowship for Intentional Communities*, last modified 1996, accessed August 2012, http://www.ic.org/pnp/cdir/1995/01kozeny.php.

Lewis, David Levering. "Two Responses to American Exceptionalism: W. E. B. Du Bois and Martin Luther King, Jr." *Black Renaissance/Renaissance Noire* Summer-Fall (2002): 8–16.

Mosley, Walter. *Futureland*. New York: Grand Central Publishing, 2002.

Nama, Adilifu. *Black Space: Imagining Race in Science Fiction Film*. Austin: University of Texas Press, 2008.

Salaam, Kalamu Ya. *What Is Life: Reclaiming the Black Blues Self*. Chicago: Third World Press, 1994.

Sandoval, Chela. *Methodologies of the Oppressed*. Minneapolis: University of Minnesota Press, 2000.

Toure. *Never Drank the Kool-Aid: Essays by Toure*. New York: N.Y. Picador Press, 2006.

Walker, Alice. *Anything We Love Can Be Saved*. New York: Ballantine Books, 1998.

Walton, Hanes. *The Political Philosophy of Martin Luther King, Jr.* Westport: Greenwood Press, 1971.

Zeiger, David. Prod. and Dir. *Sir! No Sir!* Docurama Studio, 2005. http://www.sirnosir.com/the_film/synopsis.html.

Contributors

Rochelle Brock, PhD, is an associate professor of Urban Education and executive director of the Urban Teacher Education Program at Indiana University Northwest in Gary, Indiana. She is also editor for *The International Journal of Critical Pedagogy* and series editor of Black Studies and Critical Thinking. She has written books and articles on white privilege, teacher identity, critical pedagogy, African American popular culture, and black feminist theory.

James L. Conyers, PhD, is the director of the African American Studies Program, director of the Center for African American Culture, and university professor of African American Studies at the University of Houston. He is the editor of the recently published volume, *Charles H. Houston: An Interdisciplinary Study of Civil Rights Leadership* (2012).

Lisbeth Gant-Britton, PhD, is the students affairs officer for the UCLA Interdepartmental Program in Afro-American Studies. Her book, *Holt African American History* (2007), is used in high schools and community colleges across the country. Her previous work, *African-American History: Heroes in Hardship*, won the Los Angeles Mayor's Office Special Commendation for its contribution to racial understanding through education in 1992. She teaches courses in African American history and literature. She is also an Americanist focusing primarily on narrative.

Ronald L. Jackson, PhD, is the dean of McMicken College of Arts and Sciences and professor of communication. Jackson is one of the leading communication and identity scholars in the nation and currently coeditor (with Kent Ono) of *Critical Studies in Media Communication*. His research explores empirical, conceptual, and critical approaches to the study of masculinity, identity negotiation, whiteness, and Afrocentricity. He is author of twelve books. His most recent works are *Sage Encyclopedia of Identity*, *Culturing Manhood: Global Perspectives on Masculinity and Manhood*, and *Marginalized Masculinities in the Media* (with Jamie Moshin).

Kameelah Martin, PhD, is a visiting scholar in the African American Studies program at the University of Houston. She earned her PhD in English from Florida State University in 2006. Her area of focus is twentieth-century African American literature and folklore with an emphasis on the conjuring tradition and other forms of African-centered spirituality. She is the author of *Conjuring Moments in African American Literature: Women, Spirit Work and Other Such Hoodoo* (2012). She is a member of the College Language Association, National Council for Black Studies, and the South Atlantic Modern Language Association.

Portia K. Maultsby, PhD, is Laura Boulton Professor in the Department of Folklore and Ethnomusicology and director of the Archives of African American Music and Culture at Indiana University. She specializes in African American music with a current focus on popular music and the music industry and issues of transnationalism. She is coeditor of *African American Music: An Introduction* (2006) and is completing a book manuscript, *From the Margins to the Mainstream: Black Popular Music (1945–2010)*.

Toya Roberts, ABD, is currently a doctoral student majoring in educational psychology and individual differences with emphasis on higher education administration at the University of Houston College of Education Department of Educational Psychology.

Ronald Turner, JD, is the Alumnae Law Center Professor of Law at the University of Houston John O. Quinn Law Center. Professor Turner's primary areas of expertise are in the areas of labor, employment, and constitutional law. He teaches employment discrimination, labor law, torts, constitutional law, and a course on HIV/AIDS and the law. His numerous publications include books and articles on labor and employment law issues, AIDS, and hate speech. Professor Turner was also a visiting professor of law at the College of William and Mary Marshall-Wythe School of Law and was a visiting professor of history at Rice University.

Kesha Morant Williams, PhD, is an assistant professor of communication arts and sciences at Penn State University, Berks. Prior to returning to academia she worked in media, health communication, and community outreach. Her research interests include interpersonal relationships, health communication, and popular media examined through a cultural lens. Her work is consistently presented at professional conferences such as the international, national, eastern region, and health communication conferences. Dr. Morant Williams teaches classes in research methods and interpersonal, group, family, and health communication.

Index

African American women. *See* con-
    jure women; lupus, African American
    women and
African diaspora, intentional communities
    and, 97
Africana philosophy, defining, 3
Africana womanism, defining, 3
Akbar, Na'im, 60
Alabama Supreme Court, on discrimination,
    83–84
Alexander-Floyd, Nikol G., on Africana
    womanism and black feminism, 3
Allensworth, CA, 104
alternative intentional communities, hip hop
    as, 99–102
anti-Vietnam War Movement, 98
Aptheker, Herbert, 59–60
Aronson, E., 25
Asante, A.K., Jr., 99
Asante, Molefi Kete, 60
Aurora, CO, shooting rampage, 108
autoimmune diseases. *See* lupus, African
    American women and

Batiste, Elzora (conjure woman), 10–11
Batiste, Eve (conjure novice), 9–11
Batiste, Mozelle (conjure woman), 9–10
Benlysta, 67
Bey, Yasiin, 100, 101, 102
biography disruption, identity and, 68
Black feminism, Africana womanism *vs.*, 3
Black Feminist Thought (Collins), 9–10
Black men. *See* racism at PWIs
Black Monday (Brady), 41
Black National Convention (1972), 104
Black Star
    history of, 100–101
    lyrics of, 102
Blake, Cecil, 58
Brady, Tom P. *(Black Monday)*, 41
Brocks, Rochelle, 5

Brooker, Peter, 58
Brotherhood of Locomotive Firemen and
    Enginemen, discrimination by, 81–84
Burns, Robert, 46
Butler, Octavia, fictional intentional
    communities by, 106–7

Campbell, Clive, 99
"Captain Sterling's Little Problem," 98
Carroll, Diahann, 10–11
case studies (lupus), 70–76
    grounded theory and qualitative con-
        tent analysis, 72
    group characteristics, 70–73
    themes, 73–76
    validity and reliability of, 72–73
CDC (Center for Disease Control), 66
Cell, John W., 39
Center for Intentional and Communal
    Development, 106
Chance, Julia, 99
Citizens' Council, in Mississippi, 40–42
Civil Rights Movement, 37–50
college campuses. *See* predominantly white
    institutions (PWIs)
Collins, Patricia Hill, 9–10, 12, 46
colonialism, impact on Africana culture.
    See "The Suppression of the African
    Slave Trade," analysis of
conjure women, 7–18
    challenging popular beliefs, in film,
        16–17
    conjure, defining, 17n1
    in *Daughters of the Dust*, 12–16
    in *Eve's Bayou*, 9–11
    in film, 7–8
    as folk heroes, 7
    reappropriating image of, 16–17.
    See also sexuality, in conjure women
consciencism, defining, 4
Conyers, James L., 5

Cooper, Anna Julia, as cultural motif, 3
Creel, E.M., 83
critical race theory, 24–25
cultural deficit model, of education, 49
cultural relevance, defining, 58
culture, defining, 61

D'Augelli, A.R., 22
Dark Horizons (Sargisson), 107
Dash, Julie, 8, 12
Daughters of the Dust, synopsis, 11–16
Dayton funk music, 51–55
   funk, development of, 52–53
   paralleling social change, 51
   urban centers of funk music, 53
Dead Prez, "Be Healthy" hip hop lyrics, 100
Dennis, Dave, 48–49
disruption, by lupus to identity, 73, 78
Dittmer, John, 38, 42
dropout rate, of black men at PWIs, 20–21
Du Bois, W.E.B.
   cultural perspective on slavery, 62–63
   on imperialism and greed, 48
   as scholar and activist, 60
   on skin color and person's worth, 48
   "The Suppression of the African Slave Trade," analysis of, 57–63

e-books, 107–8
Eatonville, FL, 104
embracing diagnosis of lupus, 75–76, 78
empowerment, defining, 43–45
Ethnomusicology Video for Instruction and Analysis (EVIA) digital archive project, 52
Evers, Charles, leadership style of, 44
Evers, Medgar, leadership style of, 44
Eve's Bayou, synopsis, 9–11
evolution, health changes effecting identity, 74–75, 78

fair representation, in labor practice. *See Steele v. Louisville & Nashville Railroad Co.*
family-hood *(Ujamaa),* in Mississippi, 47–49
Fanon, Frantz, on racism and culture, 2
Fields, Barbara, 39
Folkman, S., 28
Franklin, John Hope, 57, 62
Fredrickson, George, 47, 48

Freedom and Socialism: A Selection From Writings and Speeches (Nyerere), 46–47
funk music. *See* Dayton funk music
Futureland (Mosley), 107, 108

Gandy, Oscar, 2
Gant Britton, Lisbeth, 5
Gary, IN, 104
gender, defining, 1, 2
Gibbs, J.T., 27–28
Glenn, C., 68
Gordon, Avery, 95, 106
Grayson, Sandra M. *(Symbolizing the Past),* 13

hairstyles, cultural meaning of, 12–13
Hammer, Fannie Lou, 42
healing women. *See* conjure women
Herc, DJ Kool, 99
Hershberger, S.L., 22
Hieroglyphics (hip hop collective), 103–4
Higginbotham, Evelyn, 100
Higgins, Nathan, 59
Hill, Herbert, 89–90
hip hop, as intentional community, 99–102
homesteading intentional communities (of color), 103–6
Houston, Charles Hamilton, 84–86. *See also Steele v. Louisville & Nashville Railroad Co.*
Hull, Akasha Gloria, 7
Hurston, Zora Neale, 104

identity, defining, 1
information age, community and problem-solving in, 107–8
infrapolitics, defining, 43
intentional communities (of color), 95–108
   future of, in fiction, 106–8
   hip hop nation as, 99
   hip hop nation as early social justice intentional community, 99–102
   history of, 96–99
   homesteading, 103–6
   intentional residential living, 105–6
   mini-intentional communities, 102–3
intentional residential living, 105–6
intentionalism, statutory interpretation approach, 85
I've Got the Light of Freedom (Payne), 42–43
It's Bigger Than Hip Hop (Asante, Jr.), 99

Jackson, Ronald L., II, 5, 68
Jonson, Allen, 2

Karenga, Maulana, 3–4, 59
Kelley, Robin D.G., 96, 101
Kelly, Robin, 43, 44–45
King, Martin Luther, Jr., on spiritual
    communities, 97
Kitwana, Bakari, 99, 105
Kweli, Talib, 100, 101

labor unions, discrimination by, 81–90
"laying on of hands," 14–15
Lazarus, R.S., 28
Lee, Valerie, 8
Lemmons, Kasi, 8, 9–11
Lewis, David L., 97
Locke, Alain, 58
Lucas, C.P., 57
lupus, African American women and, 65–80
    description of disease, 66–67, 77
    identifying with, 67–68, 78
    identifying with, embracing disease,
        75–76, 78
    identifying with, themes, 73–75, 78
    limitations and implications, 78–79
    racial disparity of, 67, 77
    research study methodology, 69–73
    social support for, 68–69, 78
    social support systems, 76–77
Lupus Research Institute (LRI), 67

mammy figure, counter-stereotype of,
    13–14
Marable, Manning, 60, 63
Martin, Kameelah, 4–5
Maultsby, Portia, 5
Methodologies of the Oppressed (Sandoval),
    98
Mississippi movement, 37–50
    family and community, 46–47
    lessons from, 49–50
    race, in Mississippi, 39–40
    race and objectification, 39–40
    race and power, ideologies, 40, 48
    race and segregation in, 38–42, 47
    racial stereotypes, by Citizens' Council,
        41–42
    SNCC in, 42–46
Moody-Turner, Shirley, on Anna Julia
    Cooper as cultural motif, 3
Moore, James, 44

Mosley, Walter, 107, 108
Muhammad, Elijah, 106

NAACP
    civil rights struggle and, 38
    leadership of, empowerment of black
        people and, 44
    perspective of Citizens' Council, 41–42
    SNCC and, leadership styles, 44–45
Nation of Islam, black collective farming
    by, 106
Nkrumah, Kwame, 4, 47, 48
Nyerere, Julius K., 38
    Ujamaa, defining, 46–47
    Ujamaa and exploitation, 48

objectification
    and educator training about, 49–50
    empowerment and, 45–46
    race and, 39–40
Olamina, Lauren (fictional intentional
    community dweller), 107
online social support groups (for lupus),
    68–69
Outlaw, Lucius, on Africana philosophy, 3

Parable of the Sower (Butler), 106–7
Parable of the Talents (Butler), 106–7
Parker, L., 24–25
paternalism, in education, 49
Patterson, Robert, 40–42
Paulson, Lisa, 97
Payne, Charles, 42–43
Peasant, Amelia ("exoticized Other"), 12
Peasant, Nana (conjure woman), 11–14
    African-centered spirituality of, 14–15
Pep Love *(Rigmarole)*, 103
prejudice, defining, 25
public intentional communities, defining, 97
    See also intentional communities (of
        color)
purposivism, statutory interpretation
    approach, 85–86

race, defining, 1, 39–40
racism at PWIs, 19–29
    coping strategies, 20, 26–28
    critical race theory, 24–25
    differential effects and experiences of
        attending, 21
    dropout rates, 19–20, 20–21
    faculty connections, 23

frequency of, 20
perceived campus racial climate, 22–24
prejudice, defining, 25
psychological stress responses, 28
racism, biopsychosocial effects of, 26–27
racism, defining, 25–26
relation to health outcomes, 21, 28–29
social integration, 23–24
racism in South Africa, U.S. compared to, 47–48
Railway Labor Act (RLA) of 1926
Brotherhood labor union in Alabama and, 82–84
Houston's argument, U.S. Supreme Court, 84–86
U.S. Supreme Court decision, 81, 87–90
Republicanism, African Americans and, 59
Reviere, Ruth, on need for Afrocentric methodologies, 4
Rigmarole (Pep Love), 103
Riley, Raymond "Boots," 103
Roberts, Toya, 5
Royce, Josiah, 97
Rudwick, Elliott, 59

Sandelowski, M., 69–70
Sandoval, Chela, 98
Sargisson, Lucy, 107
Schaefer, Richard T., 1, 2, 58
segregation, in Mississippi, 40
self-empowerment, in hip hop, 102
separation, adaptive response to racism, 28
sexuality, in conjure women
beauty and conjuring as antithetical, 10–11
mammy image, Nana as counter-stereotype, 13–14
Mozelle Baptiste as counter-stereotype, 9–10
Simien, Evelyn M., on Africana womanism and black feminism, 3
Siple, Gillian, 106
Sir! No Sir! (2005), 98
skin color, color preference prejudices of, 11–12
SNCC (Student Nonviolent Coordinating Committee), 37–50
in Mississippi, 42–46
NAACP and, 44–45
See also Mississippi movement
social support systems, for lupus, 76–77, 78
spirituality, African-centered, 14–15

Steal This Album (The Coup), 103
Steele v. Louisville & Nashville Railroad Co., 81–90
case background, 81–84
impact of, 90
interpretive task and argument to U.S. Supreme Court, 84–87
U.S. Supreme Court's decision, 87–90
Steiner, Bernard
describing Du Bois, 59
on Du Bois's study, 63
on slave trade with Africa, 61
Stewart, James B., on Anna Julia Cooper as cultural motif, 3
Stewart, Rowena, 52
structural functionalism, defining, 58

Temple, Christel, 61
The Coup, 98, 103
"The Suppression of the African Slave Trade," analysis of, 57–63
cultural relevance, 60–63
reflexivity and cultural continuity, 63
structural functionalism, 59–60
Their Eyes Were Watching God (Hurston), 104
Tinto, V., 23
Touraine, Alain, 96
Turner, Ronald, 5

United Negro Improvement Association (UNIA), 100–101
U.S. Supreme Court
decision, *Steele* case, 87–90
Houston's petition, *Steele* case, 84–87

Van DeBurg, William L., 61

"we know what is best for you" syndrome, in education, 49
West Oakland Reconciliation & Social Healing Project (six-family cohort), 105–6
What Next (Mosley), 108
Williams, Kesha M., 5
Williams, Morant, 68
withdrawal, adaptive response to racism, 27

Yellow Mary (character, *Daughters of the Dust*), 15–16
Yetman, N.R., 26

Zeiger, David, 98

CPSIA information can be obtained at www.ICGtesting.com
Printed in the USA
BVOW08s2201030913

330076BV00006B/11/P